AUTISM
AND YOUR
TEEN

AUTISM AND YOUR TEEN

Tips and Strategies for the Journey to Adulthood

Blythe Grossberg, PsyD

AMERICAN PSYCHOLOGICAL ASSOCIATION
Washington, DC

Published by
American Psychological Association
750 First Street, NE
Washington, DC 20002
www.apa.org

APA Order Department
P.O. Box 92984
Washington, DC 20090-2984
Phone: (800) 374-2721; Direct: (202) 336-5510
Fax: (202) 336-5502; TDD/TTY: (202) 336-6123
Online: http://www.apa.org/pubs/books
E-mail: order@apa.org

In the U.K., Europe, Africa, and the Middle East, copies may be ordered from
Eurospan Group
c/o Turpin Distribution
Pegasus Drive   Phone: +44 (0) 1767 604972
Stratton Business Park   Fax: +44 (0) 1767 601640
Biggleswade, Bedfordshire   Online: https://www.eurospanbookstore.com/apa
SG18 8TQ United Kingdom   E-mail: eurospan@turpin-distribution.com

Typeset in Avenir by Circle Graphics, Inc., Reisterstown, MD
Printer: Automated Graphic Systems, White Plains, MD
Cover Designer: Naylor Design, Washington, DC

Library of Congress Cataloging-in-Publication Data
Names: Grossberg, Blythe N., author.
Title: Autism and your teen: tips and strategies for the journey to
   adulthood / by Blythe Grossberg.
Description: First Edition. | Washington, DC : American Psychological
   Association, [2018] | Includes bibliographical references and index.
Identifiers: LCCN 2018027232 (print) | LCCN 2018043802 (ebook) | ISBN
   9781433830273 (eBook) | ISBN 1433830272 (eBook) | ISBN 9781433830150
   (pbk.) | ISBN 1433830159 (pbk.)
Subjects: LCSH: Autism in adolescence. | Teenagers.
Classification: LCC RJ506.A9 (ebook) | LCC RJ506.A9 .G75825 2018 (print) |
   DDC 616.85/88200835—dc23
LC record available at https://urldefense.proofpoint.com/v2/url?u=https-3A__lccn.
loc.gov_2018027232&d=DwIFAg&c=XuwJK26h77xqxpbZGgbjkdqHiCAgI8ShbCm
Qt4IrFlM&r=jxDmcfdMwrJ1f_jnNnialA&m=bxba939-WDTcR0psgAZae4dntKYa_
XHEmdvu0oc3-9g&s=CjAAN6bjP9Yk3cgdJXWqSISFxkJb-R78JJ11E7ghscQ&e=

British Library Cataloguing-in-Publication Data
A CIP record is available from the British Library.

Printed in the United States of America

http://dx.doi.org/10.1037/0000118-000

10 9 8 7 6 5 4 3 2 1

Contents

AUTISM AND YOUR TEEN

1

Seven Messages for Parents of Teens and Young Adults on the Spectrum

This book is written to help you navigate the sometimes bumpy path of raising a child on the autism spectrum. Many books on the market discuss the initial steps of the long journey you will take guiding your child to adulthood, including your child's initial process of being diagnosed with autism and the process of getting services for your young child or school-age child. This book picks up where those books leave off and covers adolescence and the young adult years (ages 11–21 years).

The chapters herein offer guidance for parents with children all along the spectrum and with differing levels of skills. Throughout, *autism spectrum* or *autism spectrum disorder* (ASD) will be used to refer to a group of developmental differences marked by difficulty with social interaction and communication and by repetitive behaviors and restricted interests. The spectrum includes people with autism and what was formerly known as *Asperger's syndrome*. The terms *lower* and *higher functioning* refer to the degree to which a person can speak and the degree to which the person's intelligence can be measured in a conventional manner. These terms are not meant to convey moral judgment, as those with lower functioning forms of autism can also have considerable talents. I also use different pronouns to refer to your child, including *she* and *he*, but this book is also inclusive of teens and young adults who are transgender or gender fluid.

In writing this book, I want to acknowledge how complicated your children's journey to adulthood can be and how confusing, rewarding, financially staggering, and bewildering it can be for you as the parent. I also want to acknowledge that although this book provides strategies and tools, there is no one right way to raise your child. You also don't need to feel guilty if you can't follow up on these suggestions. I find that a lot of burdens are placed on parents of teens and young adults with autism, and you are often asked—by teachers, doctors, and other members of the community—to do more, while you may also be holding down one or more jobs, caring for other children or parents, and trying to pay the bills. There is always a limit to what you can do, emotionally, practically, and financially. Find the strategies that work for you, and don't burden yourself with the others. The "right" strategies are also the ones that work for you at that moment of your life. Some issues require immediate attention, and others can't be addressed right now. Realize that raising your child is a process, and part of the work involves recognizing your limitations and forgiving yourself for being human. When the time is right, you'll get to the strategies and stages that work for you and your child. In the process, some things may have to slide. For example, if you're facing high medical and other costs for one child, you may not be able to afford braces for your other one. If you're dealing with trying to get your teen to school, you may not be able to teach her to get dressed on her own. Prioritize what seems important and forgive yourself for not getting to the other tasks right now.

There are some messages that I will return to more than once in the following chapters, as I describe the path of your child's development at a more granular level. I hope that you can internalize these messages as you read and as you continue along your parenting journey. Feel free to come back to these pages any time you need encouragement.

MESSAGE #1: CHALLENGING YEARS CAN ALSO BE YEARS OF GROWTH

Kids do not always present with a linear path of development. Although this is true of all kids, it is particularly true of kids on the autism spectrum. As they grow older, kids with autism may develop a split between their intellectual skills and their life skills. This might be confusing for you as a parent, as you know in your gut that your child is capable of so much more but doesn't seem to be able to thrive in everyday situations. You aren't wrong. The discrepancy between intellectual and practical skills can be frustrating, as your child might be able to carry out amazing tasks such as multiplying three-digit numbers in her head while not being able to tie her shoes. Just because your child still struggles in certain areas, it doesn't mean she isn't growing. Even struggles represent growth, not stasis, or staying the same.

In recognizing what your child continues to need to work on as she progresses through adolescence, note what she is doing well and the ways she has progressed. It can be difficult to recognize progress when children seem to struggle with such basic skills as using money, taking transportation, or dressing themselves. It can also be tempting to compare your children with neurotypical children (children who aren't on the autism spectrum or who don't present with another form of neurodiversity or difference in a way of functioning and thinking), for whom some of these skills can be so easy. However, resist the temptation to equate difficulty with hopelessness or to lose sight of what your kids are good at. You've likely already measured growth for your child by comparing her with the way she was in previous years instead of comparing her with other children, and that's a great skill to continue. Think about your child's growth relative to what he or she did before. There will be growth, even if there are moments when it seems like your child is moving backward.

MESSAGE #2: HONOR THE STRUGGLE

Just because I'm encouraging you to look at your child's growth in a relative way, it doesn't mean that you shouldn't acknowledge the very real struggles that you and your children are going through. Preadolescence, and adolescence in particular, can be times of great struggle for children on the spectrum and their parents (though not necessarily for everyone). By suggesting that you honor the struggle, I mean that you should acknowledge how hard this time can be for you and your kids.

Be kind to yourself and them as you go through these difficult times. Recognize that while it isn't always easy, your child's struggle may represent growth. Her willingness to embrace new challenges, become more independent, and engage with others represents growth, even though these efforts might also bring complications. For example, many children with autism become more willing to understand social interactions and complications as they grow older. This represents true growth, but it also means that they also might become very frustrated as they come out of their shell and try to make sense of the world. Seeing struggle as progress may help as you go through these times of readjustment with your child.

MESSAGE #3: HONOR YOUR INSTINCTS AS A PARENT

You know more about your child than so-called experts. You are in the best position to know what your child needs and the people he or she should work with. Although you can call on experts, you will be a vital part of the process of helping your child and figuring out what she needs. Trust yourself. If you sense something isn't working, honor your instinct. If a person you're working with isn't taking the time to know your child and her history, consider switching to someone who will acknowledge your perspective as a parent and work with you as a partner. As more and more professionals are trained to work with autism spectrum disorders, you can find someone who understands the particular struggles and triumphs of a child on the spectrum and those of her family.

MESSAGE #4: YOU ARE A PERSON, TOO

It's easier said than done, but if you are fortunate enough to have a partner, spouse, parent, friend, or trusted babysitter who can help you, call on that person. Carve out time for yourself.

And when you're away from your child, don't spend the time making phone calls on his or her behalf or ruminating about his or her future. Instead, spend the time truly relaxing and being a person, whether that means sitting in a hammock reading or (because it's great to keep a bucket list) skydiving. Many parents are tempted to spend their free time writing their son's IEP (individualized education program) or calling their daughter's ABA (applied behavior analysis) therapist. Don't, if you can possibly manage it. This can be difficult for parents who have to work, not to mention parents who have to work multiple jobs, and those who are parenting solo. The chapters that follow will help you identify resources, many of them free, that can help you.

Surround yourself with people who understand. That means you might decide not to be around families who don't "get" your child. Find people who have children on the spectrum or who are sympathetic to its struggles. You'll feel empowered if you do, and you'll have sources of strength and people to call on in moments of crisis. Mindfulness training can also be a way to relish the present and to step back and see your child—and yourself—in a nonjudgmental way. Chapter 8 includes more details about how to help yourself, and in so doing, help your child.

MESSAGE #5: THERE ARE PEOPLE WHO CAN HELP

One of the most difficult things about parenting a child on the spectrum is that it can be very isolating. If you have a child who tends to throw tantrums or who can be aggressive, it can be hard to find social outlets. As a result, parents might feel that they are locked in their house. However, just as parents need to get out of the house when they can, they also need to find people they trust. The world of autism has changed in recent years so that there are doctors, therapists, and even dentists who are knowledgeable about children on the spectrum and who are set up to help them. You don't need to work with people who don't understand, and you can get the help you need.

Each step of the way, you can find people who understand your child and who won't, for example, gasp when your child has a tantrum in the waiting room or can't floss her own teeth. There are more and more children with special needs and professionals who are trained to help them. Don't settle for good enough. There are people who will not only accept your child but also celebrate his or her strengths. These are the people you should work with and who will make you feel less alone. In addition, there are more and more parents like you, eager to find a world in which people who are not neurotypical can feel comfortable. You are not alone.

MESSAGE #6: WE'RE DISCOVERING NEW THINGS EVERY DAY—THERE'S HOPE

One of the most exciting things about the world of autism spectrum disorders is that researchers and those who provide services are making new discoveries every day. In addition, as more and more kids who were diagnosed with autism as young children enter adulthood and are the beneficiaries of proven, validated treatments, we have a better sense of what they are capable of. There are now better services for young adults on the spectrum, including assistance in the transition to independent living, and there are even employers who understand the benefits of employing people at all levels of the autism spectrum. Kids are being educated in what autism is—there is now even a character on *Sesame Street* with autism—and these kids will bring this understanding with them as they get older. Try not to see your child's situation as static. What he is today is not necessarily what he will be over time.

MESSAGE #7: EXIST IN THE MOMENT

At the same time that you plan for your child's future and work as her advocate, try to exist in the moment. Children on the spectrum have a way of seeing things that few other people do. Relish their perspective, whether it's spelling words backwards or figuring out how to paint their toenails. Your child is refreshing and able to appreciate the world in a unique way. Perhaps, for example, he loves the way trucks sound or can bounce for an hour without stopping on a trampoline. Take snapshots, both visual and mental, as your kids remind you of what it's like to exist in the moment. Mindfulness techniques, including meditation, can help you slow down and quiet your own thoughts so that you are more present for your child.

WHAT'S IN THE REST OF THE BOOK

The chapters that follow will help you understand the different facets of your child's existence as they move through adolescence and young adulthood, and how you can help him at each stage. Chapter 2 provides an overview of the ways in which autism and adolescence intersect and the struggles and triumphs that many adolescents and young adults on the spectrum experience. Chapters 3, 4, and 5 cover the academic, social, and medical aspects of raising teenagers and young adults with autism, respectively, and each chapter contains stories of real parents and teens on the spectrum, as well as practical parenting strategies that are also recapped at the end of each chapter. (Names of individuals have been changed or removed to protect their confidentiality, and some stories are composites of the experiences of real people.) Chapters 6 and 7 include strategies for how to help your child with self-care and independence and how to help them move toward young adulthood. Chapter 8 gives information and strategies about how you can take care of yourself as a parent—because by taking care of yourself, you will be taking care of your child. In each chapter, I discuss the ways in which your child's development may be affecting you as a parent, because your interactions and experience are vital to the life and experience of your child. I also suggest a few practical things you can do to help your child manage the life changes he or she is going through during adolescence and early adulthood.

2

What It Looks Like When Autism and Adolescence Intersect

When Alex, a boy with high-functioning autism, turned 12, he started to worry. He couldn't quite pin down why he was so anxious, but he noticed he was outgrowing his clothing. When his dad explained that Alex would soon have a growth spurt, Alex imagined his clothing suddenly ripping apart and falling off. He wondered if he'd still be able to fit into his bed when the growth spurt happened. He also noticed that movies showed that teenagers had romantic partners. His dad told him that dating was for people over 16, so Alex made definite plans to have a girlfriend on the day after his 16th birthday.

When Madison became a teenager, she went from doing well in school and being a peaceful kid who followed the rules to being someone who became enraged and struck her siblings. Her parents did not understand her rage until they realized, after consulting a doctor, that she had developed obsessive-compulsive disorder, or OCD, which filled her mind with anxiety and the need to "act out" to rid herself of her need to repeat words and actions. Her psychiatrist said that while Madison had always struggled with some obsessions and compulsions, some of these symptoms had worsened with the onset of puberty.

BRAIN AND BODY FACTORS THAT AFFECT SPECTRUM TEENS

In the introductory story, Alex exhibits many of the wonderful eccentricities that some teens on the autism spectrum share. Although many teens with autism can easily master the biology behind the changes of adolescence, the more nuanced details of the social and emotional changes they will go through are a bit more perplexing. However, spectrum teens may be able to weather the changes of adolescence with good grace, and this can be a time of considerable growth in maturity and skills. On the other hand, Madison's experience exemplifies the often-rocky nature of adolescence on the spectrum when the hormonal, psychological, and physical changes it brings can worsen psychiatric problems and cause teens and their parents significant distress. This chapter will help you guide your teen as he or she faces the psychological changes that adolescence brings.

The path of each child through adolescence is different. For many kids on the spectrum, adolescence is a time of great maturation and improved functioning. After receiving interventions such as social skills training and organizational help, some children on the spectrum are ready to thrive as they move into their teen years.

However, some studies and anecdotal reports have found that adolescence is a time when behavioral and psychiatric issues for many kids on the spectrum spike. The reasons for this may stem from brain and body chemistry. Researchers such as Blythe Corbett and Tony Simon at the UC Davis MIND Institute have found that adolescents on the spectrum have a higher base rate of cortisol in their systems. Cortisol is a hormone that the body secretes as part of the so-called fight-or-flight response, and its elevation indicates that the body is under a significant degree of stress. Cortisol may have served a purpose in prehistoric times, as it readied the body for the speed it would need to either battle or flee an approaching angry mastodon; however, a higher level of cortisol in spectrum teens means that their bodies are always in a state of arousal and stress, leading to increased dysregulation.

In addition, approximately one quarter of people on the spectrum begin to have seizures during adolescence (rates in some studies have varied from 22% to 38%).[1] Seizure activity

---

[1] https://www.spectrumnews.org/news/risk-of-epilepsy-in-autism-tied-to-age-intelligence/

can be difficult to detect. Teens may show the effect of seizures though aggression or behavioral dysregulation rather than convulsions. *Dysregulation* refers to behavior that is outside the conventionally accepted range of behaviors; for example, hitting in response to stress is considered a form of dysregulation. Teens who are experiencing seizures might also show academic or cognitive declines. Seizures can be detected through an electroencephalogram (EEG) and must be treated. Even though most autistic teenagers do not have seizures, it's important to be alert to this possibility and seek help if you suspect seizure activity.

The practical result of this type of bodily stress is the behavior we expect from most teens—mood changes and increased emotional sensitivity. However, there are also challenges specific to spectrum kids, including increased sensory arousal, significant psychiatric issues, and behavioral challenges. For teens with autism who can't voice or can't name their confusion over the difficulties they encounter in increasingly complex social situations, the situation can become even more inflamed.

As a result of the changing nature of adolescents' bodies and brains, many psychiatric conditions can either appear or worsen during the teen years, particularly for teens on the spectrum. This does not mean that your child will develop these issues, as many spectrum teens show better functioning in adolescence than they did during early childhood or the elementary school years. However, some teens on the spectrum develop psychiatric conditions or symptoms for which they need professional help. For example, many children with autism struggle with repetitive behaviors and speech, which are core features of autism, but they may also develop full-blown OCD. OCD can develop at any age, but it can be common for pre-adolescents or early adolescents to show symptoms. Although it is difficult at times to distinguish between autism and OCD, as many of the symptoms are similar, there is also a higher risk for teens with autism to develop full-fledged OCD.

Because teens on the spectrum sometimes feel socially isolated from their typically developing peers, their risk for depression and anxiety grows, and it's important as parents to be aware of symptoms that could indicate depression or anxiety. These can include loss of interest in activities that your child normally enjoys or changes in sleeping or eating patterns. For girls on the spectrum, menstruation can also bring hormonal changes that result in obsessiveness, aggression, and/or anxiety (Chapter 6 includes more details about changes you may see when your daughter gets her period). Teens who do not receive help for these issues may try to cope with them through aggression or through dangerous behaviors such as illicit drug and alcohol use.

Although each teen's path to early adulthood is different, and there are many spectrum teens who stay mentally healthy and who flourish in adolescence, it is important to work with a doctor who is sensitive to your child and who knows about autism. It can be tricky to distinguish between the normal symptoms of autism and coexisting conditions (such as OCD or anxiety), so the physician you choose should be a good listener and well trained in autism. In Chapter 5, there is more information about working with doctors and other professionals during your child's teen years.

THE THEORY OF MIND AND SPECTRUM TEENS

In addition to going through brain and body changes, teens face an increasingly complex social world. Higher functioning teens on the spectrum might be more aware of the social stresses that surround them and the ways in which they feel socially isolated from neurotypical peers. Even though they might appear less mature than their neurotypical peers, they still have the same desires and confusions as everyone else. However, most teens on the spectrum lack the social intuition that can help guide them through these situations, making them more anxiety provoking.

Spectrum teens' misunderstanding of the way maturation works may complicate the situation even more. For example, while all teens struggle to understand how they are going to grow up to be adults and how their bodies will slowly change, spectrum teens may show less intuition about the way maturation works. Alex, in the anecdote that began this chapter, was a 12-year-old boy on the spectrum who thought that he would be able to acquire a girlfriend the day after his 16th birthday, and he was significantly worried about being able to fit into his bed after what he expected would be an overnight growth spurt. Spectrum teens who also wonder about their sexuality or whose sexuality is contrary to what is accepted by their families or extended social network may suffer additional stresses, just as many neurotypical teens who are gay, lesbian, transgender, or bisexual do.

Preteens and teens on the spectrum might have been exposed to sex education in their health classes and might understand the biological realities of their maturation, such as that they will grow facial hair or develop breasts, but they might not understand the deeper realities related to these changes. In part, this situation is a result of their slower development or relatively immature development of executive function skills. These skills, including the ability to regulate behavior and function in a cognitively flexible way, help children and adolescents develop the ability to deal with ever-changing complicated social situations. Many researchers, such as Elizabeth (Liz) Pellicano, believe that there is a connection between the immature state of executive function skills and the lack of development of what is called the "theory of mind." This is the idea that people with autism do not always understand that other people have different beliefs and thoughts than they do. In other words, people with autism tend to assume that other people think exactly as they do, and some researchers, such as Simon Baron-Cohen, one of the top scientists in the field of autism, believe that the theory of mind is the central or defining feature of autism. The maturation of one's executive functions, which are controlled largely by the decision-making front part of the brain called the prefrontal cortex, is essential to beginning to understand the complex social relationships that begin to develop during adolescence.

Therefore, the cognitive and social stresses that teens face as they think about how they will mature, develop romantic relationships, and fit in with their peers may be compounded in spectrum teens by physiological and brain factors. Teens on the autism spectrum may experience added stress and show increased receptivity to stress. In addition, outlets such as voicing their fears and worries may not be available to them, as they can't always express themselves or understand how they are feeling. This all adds up to stress for which spectrum teens may seek outlets such as aggression toward family members, the use of drugs or alcohol, or the escape into endless video games. Chapters 4 and 6 have information to help you deal with these challenges.

THE LIGHT AT THE END OF THE PROVERBIAL TUNNEL

Eventually, although adolescence for some people on the spectrum can be a time of great difficulty, cognitive development will help some spectrum teens as they age. In general, teens who struggle with symptoms of ADHD (attention-deficit/hyperactivity disorder) such as hyperactivity, impulsivity, and inattentiveness—as many people on the spectrum do—will tend to show improvement in these areas, according to researchers such as Russell Barkley. Researchers have found that over time, symptoms of hyperactivity in ADHD slowly ebb and that about one third of adults who were diagnosed with ADHD as children will not meet criteria for ADHD in adulthood. Development of the prefrontal cortex (the part of the brain that helps people with decision making and judgment), a process that many researchers believe does not end in adolescence but continues well into young adulthood, will help many teens on the spectrum who also struggle with the symptoms of ADHD. Over time, people across the spectrum may show better judgement and self-control as their brains develop in later adolescence and early adulthood.

The research has suggested that although some people who were diagnosed with ADHD as children may continue to struggle with the less visible forms of the disorder, including inattentiveness and impulsivity, the hyperactive symptoms wane over time. This means that as teens on the autism spectrum develop, they may be better able to attend to strategies that will help them regulate their behavior.

In addition, scientific and public awareness of how children on the spectrum age is advancing each year. For example, a 2016 study by Inge-Marie Eigsti found that some people who had been diagnosed with an autism spectrum disorder as children no longer met diagnostic criteria as they aged—to the point where researchers found them indistinguishable from their peers of the same age. However, young adults in the autism group tended to display what the researchers called a "broad autism phenotype" and show residual symptoms of the disorder, including trouble with shifting their attention and with communicating in a social setting. They also tended to display symptoms of ADHD, suggesting that some of the symptoms of autism remain into early adulthood in more subtle forms. These studies inform our understanding of the ways in which autism continues to affect people as they age, particularly those people on the high-functioning end of the spectrum.

These studies suggest that as high-functioning people on the autism spectrum age, they will develop the skills necessary for functioning in the adult world, even as they continue to struggle with attention and with social communication. Earlier studies painted a more dire picture of how people with autism enter the adult world, but the recent research has provided a good deal of hope that, with help, children on the spectrum can become independent adults.

The field of autism research is only beginning to benefit from longitudinal studies that track people with autism spectrum disorders over time, particularly people who benefited from empirically validated treatments (meaning treatments tested by scientific studies) as children. These studies will give us a better idea of how children who benefit from treatment fare as adults. Newer studies are also including people with different demographic variables, including a range of races, cultures, and socioeconomic backgrounds. Therefore, our knowledge of how children with autism age is constantly evolving, and this knowledge, reported in outlets such as *Spectrum News* (https://www.spectrumnews.org), helps parents know how to best guide their children toward adulthood. The explosion of research in the area of autism holds promise for our children.

HOW TO PREPARE YOURSELF AND YOUR CHILD FOR ADOLESCENCE

Although school-aged kids may not seem ready for the realities of adolescence, they are likely already being exposed to these realities in movies or through the Internet. For example, one mother who thought that no one in her child's special education school for students on the spectrum would be dating at age 13 found out that her son was very upset when a girl in his school broke up with her boyfriend in a very public way in the school bus parking lot, leaving the boy to dissolve into a tantrum. Whether teens on the spectrum truly understand what dating and relationships mean, many—even those who are in the middle or higher ranges of functioning—might have absorbed enough from popular culture and the society at large to know that it's expected of them.

It is therefore important to start preparing for these turbulent years even before your child turns 12. One way to do so is to make sure that your child is working with a good doctor, or perhaps a psychiatrist if you have insurance coverage for that type of help. Even when your child seems to be functioning well, she should visit the doctor for regular physical and mental health checkups so that your doctor can be attentive to any small changes that are occurring. It's helpful for the professionals who are working with your child to have a good baseline of her functioning before adolescence or at the beginning of adolescence so that they can notice changes in your child.

As a parent, be mindful of even small changes in your child's functioning, including increased aggression over time, that might alert you to the fact that your child's body chemistry is changing. Although there is no reason to be worried over small, periodic outbursts, significant behavioral changes that last over time should be addressed, as they may be signs that your child needs increased help or different types of interventions. For example, if your child begins to hit you or your family members regularly, a normal response would be to get angry. However, your child might be showing with his body the changes in cortisol or other hormones that come before adolescence. And even if your child looks prepubescent and acts in a way that is very immature, he or she might still be experiencing hormonal changes that will result in different behaviors and the need for help, such as psychiatric or therapeutic help.

SOCIAL STORIES

The preadolescent or early adolescent years are an ideal time to speak to your child about what he or she might experience in the years ahead. Though some of the concepts can be very difficult to understand, social stories, such as those at https://www.storyboardthat.com, can make novel social situations more comprehensible and help break them down for spectrum teens. These storyboards feature people of different races and are appropriate for a wide range of spectrum kids at different levels of language and functioning. You and your teen can use the site to build your own stories as well. For example, you can create a social story about how to strike up a conversation with a classmate (including specific behaviors that your child should carry out, such as asking a question and waiting for an answer). You can also download images from the Internet to create your own story or use photos of your child in the story. Seeing an image of themselves can help teens place themselves more readily in the social story.

Some of the concepts, such as dating, might be able to wait, but it's essential to train your teen in issues related to safety before he or she hits adolescence. It may take repeated exposure to storyboards and social stories related to dealing with strangers (such as about which types of people are safe to speak to in public) before your child starts to absorb the strategies and scripts that he or she needs. Sometimes teens might repeat the main idea of the story ("don't speak to strangers") before they understand how to apply it, so they may need even more specific guidelines—for example, in this case, about who is a stranger and who isn't. They may also have to rehearse different responses, such as not greeting a stranger in the street, before these behaviors become more natural and ingrained. Schools and ABA (applied behavior analysis) therapists can help reinforce these messages with your child so that he or she hears them from more than one place.

At first, your child might simply memorize the rules and scripts, and that's developmentally appropriate for many. It's important that your child hear these lessons long before he or she develops the type of resistance that all teens develop to their parents and that might be particularly hard to defeat in kids on the spectrum, who are also generally inflexible. Spectrum teens may lack the flexibility to use these strategies in a nuanced way, but it's important that they have some tools and strategies in their tool kits, even if these strategies are just memorized, before the teen years hit—or at least well before they are in the middle of—the maelstrom of adolescence.

When spectrum kids internalize these social strategies, they might be increasingly confused by the world around them. They will see other teenagers and adults constantly going against the rules, and this adds an extra source of frustration and confusion to their lives as developing adults. Most spectrum kids want everyone to abide by the rules, and it's important at least for parents and other adults who are close to your kids to observe simple rules, such as not swearing in public, when possible, to make your child's path a bit easier. As they develop, they might have more flexibility to understand that some rules can be broken under certain situations and others can't, but this type of understanding and nuance might take some time.

No matter how well you prepare your kids for adolescence, there is no way to ready yourself for every eventuality, and the ever-changing social landscape of adolescence will no doubt sometimes throw your kids for a loop. That is why it's so essential to have people on hand who can help.

FINDING HELP THAT FEELS COMFORTABLE TO YOU

Although autism itself is a form of neurodiversity, it is also important to ensure that the interventions and help you choose for your teen are sensitive to your cultural needs and those of your child, family, and community. Researchers such as Demetria Ennis-Cole have documented that a family's culture or traditions may influence the way they feel about their child's autism diagnosis and about the treatment they receive. Some people, such as in White American middle-class culture, tend to be more comfortable with asking for help from the medical world, whereas African Americans, Latinos, Asians, and others may feel that they can't trust the medical world or may want to solve problems on their own or within their own traditions. Single parents or those who are gay, lesbian, bisexual, or transgender may feel judged or not accepted by every medical professional. You may find that your culture and background affect the way you feel about asking for help for your child, though there is variation within different groups as well.

When you are choosing a professional to work with, it can be helpful to find someone who understands where you and your family members are coming from. Not all families respond to their child's autism diagnosis and treatment in the same way. As mentioned previously, there are often cultural variables that affect the way that you and your family members feel about getting help. It can be particularly hard if some family members feel protective and do not want to go beyond the family for help, while other members do. Some people feel more comfortable getting help in their community from people of the same ethnic background or age range or from those associated with their church, temple, or mosque or other communities they belong to. It can be hard for people to trust professionals outside their immediate circles, and starting within these trusted circles might help you or your family members if you are reluctant to ask for outside help. For example, if other members of your community or religious organization have a child with autism or a relative with autism, you can start by networking with those people to ask for referrals. If they can recommend a professional whom they trust, you might feel more comfortable with that person. Nonprofit organizations in your community may also be able to guide you. For example, Twainbow (https://www.twainbow.org) is an organization that helps provide support for people who "live under a double rainbow" as people with autism who are also lesbian, gay, bisexual, or transgender.

Although mental health professionals and physicians are not as diverse as the rest of the population, the diversity in these professions is increasing, and you deserve to work with someone who respects you and your values. Chapter 5 presents different ways you can connect with people whom you feel comfortable relying on for help with your child.

REFLECTIONS ON PARENTING

It can be difficult to watch your teen endure the triumphs and tribulations of adolescence on the spectrum, especially if he was once affectionate and relatively contented. Most parents of teens endure some trials, but it can be particularly difficult for parents of spectrum teens. The hormonal and psychological changes that puberty brings can result in psychiatric problems and dysregulation in your child, and you may feel caught off guard by your child's sudden transformation. Although all teens strive for independence, this process can be particularly fraught for your child, who may not have the maturity and skills to be independent.

Practice forgiveness of yourself and your child at each stage of the process. Reading this book can help you understand that you're not alone and that there are resources and people to help you. Take time to mourn the loss of your younger child and to celebrate the growth of your child into an adolescent. These years may be times of great growth or of growth combined with struggle, but recognize that your teen is likely finding the person she is becoming somewhat foreign too. You and your child need time to adjust to a new reality, and the tools in the upcoming chapters can help you during this period of adjustment.

PARENTING STRATEGIES

- Prepare for adolescence by having your child regularly visit a doctor or mental health professional before the teenage years so that this person can monitor your child for changes and be aware of your child's baseline behaviors.

- Monitor your child for any behavioral changes that could signify a change in your child's functioning or needs.

- Consider using social stories to help your teen develop strategies that he can use in social situations. You can use your child's picture in the social story to make it more immediate.

- Spectrum teens may lack the flexibility they need to apply social strategies in complex situations. When possible, practice the same rules yourself that you have taught your teen to observe.

- When thinking about getting help for your teen, it's helpful to acknowledge the role that your background and culture play in your feelings about getting help and to find people you feel comfortable with. Use your community to reach out to professionals with whom you will feel more comfortable.

3

Navigating the "Hidden Curriculum" in Middle and High School

Madeleine, a 10th grader with high-functioning autism, found out that she was failing several of her subjects at her mainstream public high school. Her mother found it ironic and upsetting that her daughter, who voraciously read science fiction in her free time, was failing English because she hadn't handed in any of her papers. As a requirement for her chemistry class, Madeleine had to work on a lab report with other people, but she hadn't made the time to meet and thought she'd prefer to do the lab work on her own.

Sam, who was diagnosed with autism when he was 5, was doing well in school until he reached seventh grade. He couldn't manage the sensory input of the other children, and though he used to just cover his ears and "tune out" when his environment got noisy, he now began to take out his frustrations about writing by throwing chairs and slapping his teachers. He was so distracted that he couldn't get any work done, and the school recommended that he be placed outside his district because of his behavioral issues.

THE TRANSITION TO MIDDLE AND HIGH SCHOOL

In middle and high school, scaffolding and support fall away, but many teens on the spectrum still continue to struggle with the executive function skills necessary to complete what is expected of them. Preteens and teens on the spectrum can do poorly in school, even if they are bright, because they lack the "theory of mind" (the ability to comprehend others' points of view) to understand what is expected of them, academically and behaviorally. Behaviors that might develop naturally for neurotypical kids by middle or high school do not always naturally come online for students on the spectrum.

The transition from primary or elementary school to middle school can be especially difficult for children with autism. Although primary schools can offer a certain degree of predictability, middle schools are generally larger and present students with a greater degree of sensory input and stimulation that can be difficult to manage. In addition, students have to transition from class to class and keep track of multiple assignments. At the same time, students are dealing with more complicated social situations and perhaps a sense that they don't fit in with their peers. These same demands—including the need for functional independence, sophisticated social behaviors, and sensory issues—only intensify in high school.

The sensory, academic, and social demands of middle and high school can heighten students' anxiety. The transition into middle and high school can be difficult, but there are strategies that you and your child's school can put into place to facilitate this process. You can ask that these strategies and accommodations become part of your child's IEP, or individualized educational program, during her or his last year in primary school to prepare for a smoother transition into middle and high school. This chapter will help you think ahead about what supports exist for your child's transition into middle school and other services or accommodations that might help your child going forward.

THE EXECUTIVE FUNCTION DEMANDS OF MIDDLE AND HIGH SCHOOL

Middle and high school work places a high demand on children's executive function skills—that is, their ability to plan, organize, prioritize, and change tasks flexibly as needed. Students are expected to manage more independent work than ever before. At the same time, the scaffolds and supports that students had in primary school are often taken away. For example, although it is common for teachers to place homework assignments in students' folders in primary school, students in middle school are often expected to record their own homework and complete it independently (and this is definitely true in high school). At the same time, students rotate through subject-specific teachers, who may not have the opportunity to get to know their students as well as primary school teachers do. In addition, students are forced to constantly shift their attention from one task to the next or from one subject to the next in a way that can tax students with autism, who struggle with self-regulation and flexibility. In short, at a time when kids on the spectrum need additional support, these supports are often taken away.

As discussed in Chapter 2, students with autism often struggle with executive functions. They often require reminders and step-by-step guidance from teachers to carry out what might seem like straightforward tasks. The need for support is true of students across the autism spectrum. In the example at the beginning of the chapter, Madeleine presents as a verbally gifted student whose talents don't translate into academic success because she is not motivated to direct her attention to the task at hand. Motivation can be a problem for kids on the spectrum, who are often distracted by their own inner motivations or interests and are not motivated by what the teacher presents or what their peers think is important in the classroom.

The result of executive function difficulties is that students often do not achieve results that are in line with their potential. In studying autistic students' transitions to middle school, British researchers Chantelle Makin, Vivian Hill, and Elizabeth Pellicano found that organizational aids such as plan books help students make the transition from primary to middle school. Students need explicit instruction in writing their assignments down and keeping track of when work is due. Although the goal is to eventually make them more independent, they may continue to need this assistance for longer than their mainstream peers, including into high school.

Shifting from one task to another and reacting flexibly to changes during the day can also be problematic. The typical middle and high school day, during which students travel from one classroom to another and are expected to make abrupt physical, mental, and social changes several times a day (as the students in each of their classes might be different), can be taxing for students who struggle with transitions. Students with autism may need a longer time to make these transitions and can benefit from being allowed extra time to get from class to class. They may also have trouble organizing their homework, gym bags, and other materials and may need checklists that they can follow.

SENSORY OVERLOAD

Sam, a seventh grader whose story is presented in an anecdote at the beginning of the chapter, was so distracted by sensory and social stimuli in the classroom that he couldn't attend to schoolwork. His disruptive behaviors were a result of this sensory overload.

The sensory input of middle and high school can be overwhelming. The halls and cafeteria are areas of particularly loud noises and chaotic social situations. Students with autism might become dysregulated and find it difficult to filter out excess noise and stimulation. This is also true in the classroom, which is often lit with jarring fluorescent lights and too many visual distractions.

In a mainstream school, it can be difficult to find a place for kids to have less sensory input, or to have different kinds of sensory input. At some schools, there is a "safe zone" in the nurse's office or elsewhere in which kids on the spectrum can decompress and have less sensory input of the types that make them agitated (such as loud noises) and more of the type of "sensory diet" that helps them feel calmer (such as weighted vests or blankets). At the same time, kids on the spectrum might need relaxing sensory input by being allowed to play with a soft or squeezable toy.

Students might have been comfortable wearing weighted vests or having sensory tools in the classroom in primary school, but they may feel uncomfortable wearing them in the classroom in middle or high school. The school's designated "safe spaces" might include privacy as well as other supports to help students on the spectrum become more regulated, such as a dim lighting and sensory tools.

THE HIDDEN CURRICULUM

The deficits that students with autism have related to the theory of mind (i.e., their ability to understand others' motivations and needs) can complicate their ability to navigate their way through the traditional middle or high school day. Many aspects of the school day rely on middle and high schoolers having a devel oped theory of mind. For example, students with a more developed theory of mind have a better understanding of how to handle social situations because they intuit social rules.

Many parts of the school day involve this hidden curriculum— from students' greeting each other and teachers in the morning, to being able to understand what teachers are asking on tests and in class, and knowing where to sit in the lunchroom and how to make conversation with others. In general, the less-scripted parts of the day can make students on the spectrum anxious, and sometimes they need an explicit script to follow to know how to make conversation, even if they can't handle more informal conversations.

In a more nuanced way, the academic part of the day also involves a hidden curriculum and social rules that students are expected to know how to follow. Although these rules are posted on the wall in elementary schools ("Keep your hands to yourself"), by middle school, students are expected to know what they are. However, many students on the spectrum and with ADHD (attention-deficit/hyperactivity disorder) may be socially immature and may not know what these rules are. They may also not understand teachers' directions (such as, provide "full answers with details") or be able to work well with others. Projects in which students' grades are partially determined by group work in which they struggle may also be problematic.

Students on the spectrum benefit from having these kinds of implicit rules made more explicit. For example, teachers can provide them with model answers, so students know concretely what's expected of them on different types of assessments. Teachers can also provide students with rules about how to interact with others when providing feedback or working in groups so students on the spectrum have explicit rules to follow. In general, students on the spectrum benefit from having the hidden or implicit curriculum made more explicit or direct and on the surface. Incidentally, this type of support is helpful for many kinds of students, including those with ADHD or who are socially immature, particularly during the formative years of middle school.

Students on the spectrum also benefit from clear routines and schedules. Days that contain interruptions in the schedule, such as parties, concerts, career days, field trips, and field days, are often the most confusing for kids on the spectrum, as these days involve a greater degree of ability on the part of students to understand what they need to do without explicit direction. For example, a student has to understand that on a career day, he will hear presentations from professionals in the community and be able to walk around the gym to ask questions. Students on the spectrum benefit from knowing about the schedule and getting explicit instructions about these types of days in advance.

LEARNING ISSUES

Research has suggested that there is still a difference between the academic potential and academic achievement of students with high-functioning autism. Though many students with autism have clear academic talents, they can't always achieve results in school that are in line with their talents. This is partly because many students with autism have executive function issues, ADHD, and anxiety that cause them to be distracted.

A compilation of studies looking at the learning issues of students with autism by Peggy Schaefer and G. Richmond Mancil found that although the struggles of students with autism are distinct among special education students, they face struggles nonetheless. Each student's profile is different, but many students with autism have strong math, reading, and spelling skills. They tend to be good at figuring out patterns, such as the decoding that makes up spelling or reading. However, students may struggle with graphomotor skills and writing output. In part, their problems with theory of mind complicate their social comprehension when reading (particularly fiction) and their ability to carry out social reasoning. They may also struggle with attention and complex language processing.

Students with autism may therefore present with an uneven profile, or even "splinter skills" (which are isolated skills in certain areas such as spelling or math calculations). They may be excellent at decoding, or sounding out the phonemes in words, but they may struggle to understand a more complex story. As noted previously, reading comprehension in part demands a sophisticated theory of mind and the ability to understand characters and the writer's motivation. Much is left unsaid or unwritten in more sophisticated types of writing, and students on the spectrum may need help understanding inferences. Writing can be particularly demanding, as both marshaling one's thoughts and presenting them in an organized way put a heavy demand on a student's executive functions. In addition, students may struggle with oral or complicated directions. Students with autism may enjoy the study of math or computers, yet they may struggle with word problems.

Students can benefit from being provided with visual cues and directions. For example, they may need help breaking down word problems in math and may need explicit strategies for writing (such as, begin your sentence by answering the question). Tools such as graphic organizers, in which students draw or sketch out the relationships between ideas, can help students organize and process their ideas before writing.

If feasible, communicate with your child's teachers about his personal interests, or help your child think of appropriate ways to express his interests in class. Good teachers know how to motivate students by building on their interests. For example, a student on the spectrum might be more motivated to write a paragraph about modes of transportation than about his recent vacation, so it will benefit him if his teachers offer options for writing topics.

Special education teachers, speech and language pathologists, and learning specialists can provide these types of assistance. If you feel that your child's school is not providing the types of accommodations that would help him or her access the curriculum, these strategies and strengths can be explicitly spelled out in the student's IEP. A strengths-based IEP is designed to help teachers, students, and parents recognize what a student is doing well and to build on these strengths as part of a "growth mind-set."

Sometimes students must attend special education schools to be able to access the curriculum. Teachers in these schools have training in modifying the curriculum so that students can develop their skills. Some of these schools also have 1:1 support for students and provide spaces with less overwhelming sensory input and more comforting sensory input, in addition to services such as counseling, occupational therapy, and speech-language therapy (these can also be provided in a mainstream public school). If you wish to place your child in a special education school, you will need to work with your local school board and may also need the help of a lawyer or advocate. For more information, an organization such as Autism Speaks (https://www.autismspeaks.org/family-services/tool-kits/iep-guide) can be helpful. There you can find tips for navigating the IEP process.

Students with autism can add a great deal to a classroom, and they are also capable of high achievement, particularly in areas related to STEM (science, technology, engineering, and mathematics). They can also achieve in areas such as art, music, and design, among others. The general profile of students with autism does not mean that autistic students can also not achieve in areas such as writing and literature. Many students on the spectrum are fascinated by learning languages. However, students with autism tend to enter STEM fields. For example, Paul Shattuck and colleagues at Washington University in St. Louis found that whereas 23% of the general population majors in these fields, an estimated 34% of students with autism who attend college select to major in a STEM field.

Students with autism have a great deal to add to the future of technology, especially because neurotypical students often choose not to major in STEM fields. It is necessary, however, to provide substantial academic and behavioral support to students with autism in the classroom to help them reach their potential. In addition to the humanitarian benefits of doing so, our society and economy as a whole can benefit from nurturing students who are interested in science and math and whose ability to recognize patterns can be of help to employers.

BUILDING ON YOUR CHILD'S STRENGTHS

You and your child's teachers are in the best position to help your child develop her strengths in adolescence. Though the school system may concentrate on your child's challenges, a school that is a good fit for your child will also work to develop her strengths.

Some of the strengths of kids on the spectrum include their honesty, ability to follow rules (though others are more prone to not understanding or following social rules), ability to recognize patterns, and ability to understand certain topics that interest them in depth. Encouraging their interests and encouraging their social assimilation, however, can sometimes be at odds. For example, an eighth-grade boy with high-functioning autism at a mainstream school came up with a "subway rap" because he was so compelled by the recorded voices on different subway trains. The teachers at his school encouraged him to perform his rap, but the reception from his middle school peers was mixed. Many of them laughed, but it wasn't clear whether they were laughing out of a sense of camaraderie or a sense of ridicule, and he was forever tagged as the "subway rapper" until he went to a new high school that had a special program for kids on the spectrum.

There are ways, however, to encourage the talents and tendencies of spectrum kids. Spectrum kids often do well when they are assigned specific roles in classroom activities (for example, as the reader or timekeeper), which cuts down on their anxiety about open-ended tasks. They can also be the class speller or fulfill some other role, such as artist, that calls on their talents. For example, during an obstacle course on field day at a mainstream school in ninth grade, other students had to run races or do "nonsense drills" such as stacking a tower of plastic cups as quickly as possible. The students selected their team member with high-functioning autism to take pictures of all of them, which was another task during the obstacle course. He excelled at this task, and his team members appreciated how his artistic talent contributed to the team effort.

ABA THERAPY

ABA (applied behavior analysis) therapy can be helpful at this age. Although many people think of ABA only in the context of helping younger kids, older children with autism can also benefit from the help of an ABA therapist in several ways. Research such as that by Geraldine Dawson and Karen Burner has suggested that interventions that target adolescents' behaviors can improve their social skills and adaptive behavior and result in a decrease in aggression and anxiety. Behavioral interventions, along with medication, were found to be more effective in reducing aggression than medication alone.[1] To find an ABA therapist in your area, visit the Behavior Analyst Certification Board website (https://www.bacb.com).

An ABA therapist can help break down the many complicated tasks involved in the day of a middle or high school student with autism. These types of interventions can help students feel greater confidence, develop greater independence, and reduce their frustration. There are many points in the day of a middle school or high school student into which a behavioral specialist can intervene. Consider some of the following scenarios:

- A student cannot open his or her locker because his or her fine motor skills make it difficult to do so, resulting in frustration.

- A student is confused about how to ask to sit at a lunch table.

- Overcome by loud noises, a student needs a safe space in which to take a break.

- A student can't follow the changing schedule that rotates each day.

- Not knowing how to approach other students, a student finds him- or herself not connecting with others.

- A student does not know how to pack his or her gym clothes for the next day.

By helping students break down tasks (such as each step in opening a locker) or creating a list that students can follow on their own, ABA therapists can help students develop skills and independence.

---

[1] https://www.kennedykrieger.org/patient-care/centers-and-programs/neurobehavioral-unit-nbu/applied-behavior-analysis/scientific-support-for-applied-behavior-analysis

RESIDENTIAL PROGRAMS

Sometimes it is necessary to place a child or teen with autism spectrum disorder into a residential program. This is not an easy step for a parent to take, but it may be helpful for both the parent(s) and the child if the child needs intensive therapeutic support or is too aggressive for the home. In addition, single parents or those without extended support networks or other resources may find it difficult to care for a child at home.

If you decide to place your child in a residential school, there are several factors to consider, and you may want to work with an advocate to help you find the right placement for your child. The school you select should provide 24/7 medical care to ensure that your child's medical and pharmacological needs are met, and the school should also provide intensive therapeutic support that is supervised by a doctor or psychologist. Before your child attends the school, the staff should show you a detailed and tailored plan of the ways in which they will meet your child's therapeutic, medical, cognitive, and academic needs. They should also share with you how you will be involved as a parent. You should also speak with parents and children at the school to get a sense of whether it's a good fit for your child.

SELF-ADVOCACY

Two important components of preparing students with autism for independence include identity formation and self-efficacy, according to research by Shattuck and colleagues published in the journal *Autism Research and Treatment*. Identity formation, which is important for all young adults, is the lifelong process of thinking about and refining one's identity based on race, gender, ethnic background, and disability identity. These different factors that relate to identity formation can also interact; for example, race can affect the way in which students on the spectrum see themselves. In Shattuck and colleagues' study, Black college students on the spectrum had lower self-efficacy related to getting others to listen to them, suggesting that not all students on the spectrum are the same with regard to self-efficacy and that other factors, such as race and gender, can affect the self-efficacy beliefs of a student on the spectrum. Self-efficacy is related to one's belief that they can do something.

Identity formation related to a disability can be tricky, as parents and teachers want to instill the idea in students that their cognitive and social profiles are not necessarily a disability. There has been a great deal of research about the benefits conferred by disabilities, including autism. However, students have to develop a sense of their needs to be able to ask for support that will help them become successful and independent in academic and other settings.

Self-efficacy and independence in middle and high school students can have several components. These include some of the following:

- knowing how to find answers to their questions;

- asking for extra help when needed;

- asking for accommodations in their school day, such as having extra time to get to class or wearing headphones in busy, loud spaces such as the cafeteria or auditorium;

- making sure teachers and administrators listen to them; and

- reporting bullying.

Developing one's identity, including one's disabilities, starts during adolescence, but it is a process that lasts a lifetime. Some students are helped by being part of their IEP meetings and being an active part of their transition meetings (different states have different rules about when these transition meetings start; see Chapter 7 for more information). If students eventually become part of their transition meetings, they are part of the process of envisioning their future and setting goals, increasing their motivation to achieve their goals.

Having kids write their own IEP goals can be a remarkably formative experience for kids, teachers, and parents alike. When students formulate their own goals, the goals are more likely to be meaningful to them. Parents and teachers also begin to think more concretely about what matters to the student.

In the process, parents can help their children by continuing to ask them to voice what they need and coaching them about how to ask for what they need. It's not always necessary for students to identify as having a disability, but they should be coached in asking for help. As students age, it is particularly important for parents to help them, if possible, to ask for help on their own.

There is a vital and critical difference in providing help for one's child and coaching a child to ask for help on her own. Consider the differences in the following scenarios.

Scenario 1:

- The parent of an eighth-grader meets with a teacher to explain why her son did badly on a test. OR . . .
  - The parent first asks the student to speak with the teacher directly and then follows up with the teacher, and later:
  - A student meets with a teacher and then reports back to the parent what the teacher said and what the student needs to do differently on the next test.

Scenario 2:

- The parent chooses which goals a student will select for the upcoming semester in her speech-language sessions. OR . . .
  - A parent consults with a student to develop appropriate goals, and later:
  - A student comes up with her own goals for the upcoming semester based on a deep understanding of what she wants and needs to work on.

Scenario 3:

- A parent organizes all the papers that a child brings home. OR . . .
  - A parent works with a child to place the papers back in the right folders, and later:
  - A student manages her own papers and places them in the correct folders.

Reframing these scenarios a little bit, you can think of each goal (the student taking initiative) as a progression of steps, the first step of which is parent management. The division of each goal into three steps illustrates the way in which developing independence is a progression. Although I've provided three steps in the progression toward independence, in reality there are more than three steps. The idea is for parents to begin coaching students so that the students have an awareness of their own needs, goals, and development and feel comfortable asking for help. The more students do on their own, the greater their sense of self-efficacy, which is a belief in their ability to handle whatever comes next. Well-intentioned parents want to dive into situations to save their children, but students must begin to advocate on their behalf over time, if possible, to work toward the increasing independence required in young adulthood.

REFLECTIONS ON PARENTING

As a parent, you have the natural inclination to protect your child from the inevitable bumps involved in moving toward maturity and independence. Your child's transition to middle and later high school may be marked by considerable frustration if he is not ready to carry out the more independent work that may be expected of him. Your first response may naturally be to want to slow down the process and to protect him. Over time, working with his teachers, you can transition from doing the work of organizing your child yourself toward coaching him to do it on his own. This work is a progression and does not happen overnight, but it's important to learn how to step back and help your child through coaching (e.g., helping him organize and pack his own backpack) rather than doing it yourself.

PARENTING STRATEGIES

- Find out if your child's school has safe spaces where children can go to protect themselves from sensory overload and where they can receive calming sensory input.

- Look at your child's school calendar and review with her any upcoming changes in routine for that week or that day, such as testing days, field trips, and special assemblies.

- Familiarize yourself with your child's learning profile. Common strengths include reading (decoding), spelling, and math, and common weaknesses include language processing, graphomotor skills, writing, and distractibility.

- Use the school or other support networks to find tools such as graphic organizers to help your student produce writing.

- Use the assistive technologies explained at UC Davis MIND Institute (https://www.ucdmc.ucdavis.edu/mindinstitute/) to help your child communicate.

- Help your child think of ways to share his or her strengths and develop them in the classroom, but be aware that sharing can make students the targets of ridicule by their peers.

- Consider ABA therapy to help your child develop skills to approach multistep or complicated social situations that develop in school. ABA therapy can help students at any point of the autism spectrum and at any age.

- Coach your child about how to advocate for himself. Doing this will help him build the necessary identity formation and self-efficacy that will enable him to ask for what he needs as he gets older.

4

Handling the Social Aspects of Adolescence on the Spectrum

When Rafael turned 13, he had some of the behaviors you'd expect of any teenager. He was moody and disagreed with most of what his parents said. However, his interests stayed the same as ever. While kids his age were listening to rap music and beginning to develop an interest in dating, he continued to be fascinated by trains and TV shows for kids half his age. Nothing made him as happy as watching *Scooby Doo* and *Paw Patrol* or fiddling around with his trains, and he wasn't at all interested in the way he looked. His parents weren't sure whether he was bullied, but it was clear that the kids in his mainstream school never invited him anywhere outside of school.

Destiny, who had always been a bookworm and a movie buff, was 15 when she decided to start watching television shows to develop an idea of how to become a teenager. Watching shows like *Gossip Girl*, *Black-ish*, and *Pretty Little Liars* was her way to understand what teens did. She tried to turn herself into what she saw on television, wearing a lot of misapplied makeup and gossiping about boys. She also posted very personal information on her Facebook page. As a result, she offended people and made herself feel even more uncomfortable in social situations.

THE CHALLENGES OF ADOLESCENCE AND THE RISK OF ISOLATION

As children with autism enter adolescence, they often become more interested in socializing and forming social relationships. However, their relative immaturity and relatively undeveloped "theory of mind" (the ability to comprehend others' point of view) can make it hard for them to fit in with their peers.

Younger children with autism do not tend to engage in imaginative or social play, and these deficits continue to affect kids on the spectrum as they age. Playing with peers in lower grades is a precursor to understanding the more complex social interactions of older kids. Although higher functioning students with autism spectrum disorders often develop more interest in joining social activities, they still often have core deficits and less practice than their peers in social interactions.

Many teens with autism become more aware of the ways in which they are socially marginalized, worsening their sense of isolation and feelings of anxiety and depression. They also run the risk of being bullied. Lower functioning children with autism may remain in special education classrooms where they are somewhat protected from the social pressures of their neurotypical peers, but preteens and teens with higher functioning autism are often in mainstream settings in which they become painfully aware of their social shortcomings. Because these types of students are often particularly intelligent, they sense that they do not measure up to their peers, and their self-regard suffers as a result. The dangers of social media and the Internet are magnified for spectrum teens, and they may increase their social isolation by posting inappropriately on the Internet or by not being part of online communication among other kids (for more information about Internet safety, see Chapter 6).

In my experience, some kids on the spectrum do not want to become like teenagers and resist teenage activities, maintaining the activities of younger kids. They may develop an interest in smaller kids or speak about themselves as though they were younger in an attempt to stay little. Others may decide to regard teenage things with disdain and remain "old souls" throughout adolescence. Like Rafael in the vignettes that began this chapter, some spectrum kids are frightened by adolescence. They may not understand the subtle ways in which teens change over time, and they may assume that people develop from children to adults overnight. They may require social stories to understand how people change slowly over time, and even higher functioning kids may not be intuitive about the changes in adolescence.

Finally, other preteens or teens on the spectrum may develop an interest in social interactions and try, like Destiny in the anecdotes that began this chapter, to use popular media or stereotypical behaviors to fit in with their peers. Although many teenagers (even those without autism) resort to stereotypical behaviors or base their behaviors on popular media, including shows or magazines, teens with autism can apply these stereotypes in ways that are particularly awkward and lack nuance.

SOCIAL SKILLS TRAINING

Teenagers with high-functioning autism can still struggle with many core social deficits, including the inability to make eye contact, carry out reciprocal conversations, and respond to questions in appropriate ways. Their social skills deficits can affect their interactions with peers and adults. They may also struggle with emotional regulation and the ability to develop friendships. These struggles can continue into adulthood if teens do not receive explicit training in social skills.

Social skills training for autism tends to focus on three aspects, according to research by Jeanie Tse and colleagues. These types of training are aimed at verbal, relatively higher functioning adolescents with autism. The first type of training involves using social stories or other means of making the implicit rules of the hidden curriculum more explicit (i.e., making social rules that people are expected to understand and that people with autism may not understand more explicit and clear). The second type of intervention includes "social autopsies" that help teens dissect social situations and learn from them using positive reinforcement. Other interventions use social scripts to help teens practice social situations or involve activities, such as role-plays, to improve teens' theory of mind. Theory of mind training, based on the work of British autism researcher Simon Baron-Cohen, focuses on helping people with autism recognize emotions and understand more complex mental states such as lying and humor. In this training, participants first recognize emotions and then are asked to identify the feelings of others in increasingly complicated social and emotional situations.

Different types of social skills training target different components of social interactions, from making eye contact, to starting conversations, to listening to other people, to dating skills. Research has suggested that social skills training can help adolescents with relatively high-functioning autism and that, in some cases, teenagers who receive this type of training can apply the social skills they learn to real-life situations. One validated program for teaching social skills to adolescents is the Program for the Education and Enrichment of Relational Skills (PEERS) developed at the University of California, Los Angeles. This program and other similar programs offer live models of social interaction. They use a face-to-face, real-time format in which trainers and trainees are in the same room. The social thinking curriculum developed by Michelle Garcia Winner and Pamela Crooke helps people interpret the behaviors, thoughts, and emotions of others and to react in a way that helps a person achieve his social goals. For more information, visit https://www.socialthinking.com.

However, because autism at its root involves the desire to systematize, it can be hard for teens who undergo this type of training to be able to use it in flexible and nuanced ways. That is, teens with autism like to follow rules and learn hard-and-fast guidelines that they can use in every situation. The complex and fast-paced social situations that might develop in real life defy rules and scripts, so although some of the more basic skills (making eye contact, practicing greetings) can generalize to other situations, it can be hard for people with autism to develop the flexibility to use social skills training in more complicated situations. Therefore, you and your child might also want to work with other strategies, such as video modeling, described next.

VIDEO MODELING

Video modeling has been shown to be an effective way to teach behavioral skills to children with autism, according to research by Marjorie Charlop-Christy and colleagues. Studies have shown that children with autism who watch video and live models are more able to acquire skills and better able to transfer these skills to real life than those who receive social skills training as described previously. These studies showed that children with lower functioning and higher functioning autism could learn from video modeling, although the children could not generalize, or apply the behaviors to real-life situations, when they were watching live models. These behaviors included skills such as greeting others, making conversation, carrying out independent play, and carrying out independent skills like brushing one's teeth.

Researchers hypothesize that video behavior modeling is more effective than live modeling because children with autism may attend to certain parts of live stimuli, such as the models' clothing, without attending to the models' target behavior. They also think that video modeling might improve children's motivation to learn and apply skills. Children with autism associate screens with leisure and enjoy repeating words and phrases that they hear on television or in video games.

VIDEO GAME ADDICTION

Although video modeling can be helpful, video games can be a source of frustration for parents. If your child on the spectrum spends more time playing video games or watching TV and movies than she does interacting with peers or carrying out other activities, she is not alone. This is a common problem among children with autism.

Studies have shown that children with autism are more likely to become addicted to video games than their neurotypical siblings. This suggests that autism itself, rather than the home in which a child is raised, can make that child highly likely to become addicted to playing video games. In one sibling study, children with autism spectrum disorders spent more time playing video games and watching television than they spent in all other activities. The boys spent 2.4 hours per day playing video games (vs. 1.6 hours for their typically developing siblings), and the girls spent 1.8 hours per day playing video games (vs. 0.8 hours for their typically developing siblings). They spent very little time on social media or playing video games that involved social interaction.

Video games are highly reinforcing of the tendencies of children with autism to want to control their reality and to want to handle reality with rules. These tendencies can help attract them to video games, and video games can in turn perhaps reinforce these tendencies. Research has also shown that boys with autism who have addictions to video game also have problems with attention and oppositional behavior. Role-playing games were particularly problematic.

Researchers such as Micah Mazurek, the author of these studies and a professor at the University of Virginia, believe that video games can be a way for children with autism to learn social skills, although research in this area is still developing. Some video games, such as Rock Band, require players to work together to simulate different players in a musical group. This is only one example of a game in which players have to cooperate and interact. There are other examples, which parents can investigate through sites such as Commonsense Media (https://www.commonsensemedia.org) that encourage social skills. Commonsense Media reviews help parents understand video games (and other forms of technology) by providing overviews of the games and ratings about their level of violence and their positive messages. However, playing video games can not replace actual social interaction, which is critical for teens and young adults on the spectrum.

If you are struggling to curtail your child's gaming, you are not alone. One strategy is to use video games as a reward for other behaviors you want to reinforce, such as socializing with others. If your child makes an effort to attend a club meeting or sports game, for example, he or she can be allowed to play video games for a preassigned amount of time. Another option is to allow your child to play video games if he or she has a friend over. This type of activity will give her something well-defined and structured to do, and your child will be sharing the experience with a peer. Playing games together online (during which your child is playing with kids who are in other locations) is not a form of socializing, but being in the same room as another person and offering them the choice of game allows your child to practice some social skills.

PEER-TO-PEER STRATEGIES TO IMPROVE SOCIAL SKILLS

Schools can pair students on the spectrum with typically developing "buddies" or peer models to help them navigate the school day. Buddies can help spectrum kids find their way safely from class to class and have a place to eat lunch. Some programs involve training neurotypical kids so that they can provide safe opportunities to socialize with peers.

Higher functioning spectrum kids can find like-minded peers by joining activities they like. Drama clubs may be a place where kids are more tolerant of different behaviors and abilities, and kids who don't like to act can be stage managers or work on costumes or the set. Girl Scouts and Boy Scouts also provide structured activities that are welcoming to kids on the spectrum.

Some communities also have adaptive sports programs so that kids on the spectrum can participate in sports. Although some spectrum kids have problems with gross motor skills, others do not but still have distractibility and social comprehension issues that interfere with their ability to play on a team. Today's typically developing kids also tend to specialize in a single sport at a young age and play on teams that are highly competitive, such as travel teams. These teams, which many argue put kids at risk for overuse injuries and emotional trouble such as burnout and depression, also preclude the participation of kids who need more support in understanding how to play, unlike the community sports in years past.

Some studies by Robert Koegel and others have shown that high school students on the spectrum have done well by starting a club that corresponds to their interests (such as movies, basketball, or video games). By participating in these clubs with typically developing peers, the students on the spectrum were able to improve their levels of engagement with peers and their initiation of social exchanges. These activities build on teens' motivation by having them engage with peers in an area that interests them, and the activities are also highly structured and mediated by an adult. Therefore, these types of activities require less motivation and flexibility than other types of more open-ended social activities.

The research described previously suggested that spectrum teens' interests can be the best conduit to getting them involved with peers. What they chose as their method of interaction was not important; what was important was that they chose something that compelled them to participate with peers. Even if your child's main interest is video games, this interest can provide a way to connect with peers in engaged ways.

Destiny, in the anecdotes that started the chapter, worked on makeup for the drama club at her school. Her drama teacher helped her learn how to apply makeup, and Destiny was able to connect with peers who were actors and managers in the drama club. She learned to interact in more genuine ways than she had by relying on television shows with stereotypical portraits of teenagers.

READING LITERATURE TO IMPROVE SOCIAL SKILLS

As noted in Chapter 3, reading literature can be difficult for spectrum kids. Though some are great appreciators of literature, others find it hard to understand the social motivations of fictional characters. The original 1985 experiment by Simon

Baron-Cohen and his colleagues that tested young children's theory of mind showed why. This experiment (called the "Sally-Anne test" after the dolls used in the study) involved three groups of children—neurotypical children, children with Down's syndrome, and children with autism—observing two dolls. The experimenters showed one doll placing a marble into a basket, and then another doll transferred this marble to a box. The children in the experiment were then asked where the first doll would look for the marble. Both typically developing children and children with Down's syndrome were able to state or point to the basket where the first doll had left the marble. Only autistic children (who were older in chronological age than the typically developing children in the study) indicated that the first doll would look for her marble in the box.

This study points to the idea that it's very hard for students with autism to practice the perspective-taking necessary to comprehend and enjoy literature. However, reading literature, with support, can be a way for some kids on the spectrum to develop their ability to engage in social interactions and enlarge their imaginations. Research by Diana Tamir and colleagues suggested that reading fiction can improve the theory of mind of autistic children and teens. People who read the most fiction tend to have the strongest theory of mind. Reading fiction forces the reader into the mental space of the protagonist in an intimate way that TV shows and movies generally do not, and practice reading literature can improve one's ability to understand the perspectives of others.

Choosing books for your teen or tween with autism spectrum disorder can be difficult. Your school or town librarian can help. There are also a number of well-written young adult novels in the market today in which the protagonist has a form of autism. One of the best is *The Blue Bottle Mystery* by Kathy Hoopmann, which involves elements of fantasy and reality as the main character deals with the travails of having Asperger's syndrome. Readers who are on the spectrum might, for example, appreciate the main character's tantrum when his teacher breaks his special ruler.

THE IMPORTANCE OF SOCIALIZING
AS A TRANSITION TO ADULT LIFE

Social skills training is essential because teens with autism spectrum disorders who do not find ways to socialize with their peers are at risk of feeling isolated as young adults. Learning how to engage in social interactions helps their transition to young adult life, whether that involves working or attending college. Being part of the community and learning how to engage with the community are as crucial to their eventual success as their academics. Teens who do not learn how to carry out social interactions run the risk of feeling increasingly isolated as young adults, when the structure of school ends.

REFLECTIONS ON PARENTING

It can be difficult as a parent to know when to push your child and when to accept her individuality. Many spectrum teens maintain that they are content being isolated and do not want to make the effort to socialize with others. This attitude places you in a considerable bind as a parent. On one hand, you know that socializing will help your teen move into young adulthood as someone who is likely to be better connected with her community. On the other hand, it's hard to push your teen to socialize when she simply may not want to—or doesn't know how to. Look for ways to nudge her along, such as socializing in an area of interest (for example, gaming, art, or drama). By using an area of interest to connect, she may feel more comfortable and less resistant to spending time with her peers.

PARENTING STRATEGIES

- As you encourage your teen to connect with peers, consider limiting her use of the Internet and social media, as excessive use of social media can worsen her sense of isolation and provide her with poor role models about how to socialize with others.

- To help your teen, you can try social skills training, video modeling, or a combination of training types. To get an idea of what social thinking training involves, check out this website (https://www.socialthinking.com/).

- If your child plays video games, use media ratings, such as those provided by Commonsense Media, to select games that are more prosocial in their messages and can encourage your child to at least socialize by having a friend over while gaming.

- Encourage your child to increase social interaction with others by starting lunchtime or after-school clubs at school that cater to his specific interests.

- Ask your school or public librarian to recommend young adult book titles that expose readers to different perspectives. Read and discuss fiction with your teen—ask questions to help your child understand characters' motivations, such as "Why is the character upset after her friend tells her secret to others?"

5

Finding Health Care for Your Teen or Young Adult

When Jenny's son, David, turned 18, she had to rush him to the hospital for an emergency appendectomy. Though he had just turned 18 the month before, the staff in the hospital would not permit Jenny to accompany David beyond the waiting room because her son was over 18. However, David was nonverbal and could not make his needs or history known to the doctors and nurses.

When he was 5 years old, Trevor was treated by a physician in his rural town who prescribed an antihistamine when Trevor couldn't sleep at night. The antihistamine helped Trevor fall asleep, but he often awoke 2 hours later with night sweats and crying. Trevor used sign language to communicate with his parents, who knew that his stomach was bothering him on many nights. His parents put together the idea that their son's consumption of milk products led to stomach upsets, which made Trevor wake up after the antihistamine wore off. After eliminating these foods from Trevor's diet, his sleep greatly improved, and he was able to stop taking the medication. However, now that Trevor is a teenager, he often chooses his own food at school, and he eats food that worsens his gastrointestinal issues. Although his parents have warned him against choosing foods that inflame his stomach, Trevor does not always listen to them.

FINDING THE RIGHT MEDICAL CARE

Experts, using data from the National Health Interview Survey, have found that children with autism spectrum disorder (ASD) have complicated health needs but that their primary care doctors are not always trained to meet these needs. Studies have also found that children with autism have a greater number of health and psychiatric needs than other children, as well as behavioral issues related to other health conditions. The result is that children with autism tend to have health care needs that are not met. This chapter will help you treat health-related issues that may develop in your teen or young adult child.

COMMON HEALTH CARE CONDITIONS
FOR CHILDREN AND TEENS WITH AUTISM

There are several health conditions that commonly occur in children and teens on the spectrum, in addition to the psychiatric issues discussed in Chapter 2 such as ADHD (attention-deficit/hyperactivity disorder), anxiety, depression, and OCD (obsessive-compulsive disorder). Many of these conditions worsen behavioral and other symptoms associated with autism.

According to surveys, about 46% to 85% of children with autism have gastrointestinal problems, including constipation and diarrhea.[1] In one study conducted by Karoly Horvath and Jay Perman, 84.1% of children with autism had at least one gastrointestinal symptom, including diarrhea, constipation, gaseousness, and other symptoms. The rate among their typically developing siblings was 31.2%. In this same study, half of the patients with autism had sleep disorders, whereas only 6.8% of their siblings did, suggesting that gastrointestinal problems can also result in sleep disturbances.

---

[1] https://www.autismspeaks.org/sites/default/files/docs/about_autism_0.pdf

There is ongoing research into whether food allergies cause or worsen autism. Some studies have found elevated levels of food and respiratory allergies in children with autism. Although the evidence has not been conclusive yet, some research by Paul Whiteley and colleagues suggests that people with autism can benefit from a gluten-free and/or casein-free diet. Casein proteins are found in milk. Studies on the link between autism and nutrition are ongoing and may soon lead to some results that can help doctors identify a better diet for some of their patients on the spectrum.

Gastrointestinal issues can at times result in aggressive behaviors, as children with autism can have a hard time relating the way they feel, or these issues can result in behaviors such as rocking to soothe oneself. If your child has symptoms such as constipation, diarrhea, pain in the abdomen, or vomiting on a frequent basis, you should ask your doctor for a referral to a gastroenterologist, preferably one familiar with ASD. Sometimes, treating these conditions can result in an improvement in symptoms and in aggressive behaviors.

ABA (applied behavior analysis) therapists traditionally rely on treats such as sweets and candies to motivate and reward kids. However, these treats can cause weight gain, especially when coupled with medications that are often used to treat behavioral issues in kids on the spectrum, and these treats can worsen gastrointestinal issues in some kids with food allergies or sensitivities. It's sometimes helpful to transition kids to being rewarded by other means, such as videos, video games, or bouncing on a trampoline (or whatever they will respond to that is safe).

Inflammation and allergies in children and teens on the spectrum may also surface in skin conditions. People with autism are 1.6 times more likely to have eczema and other skin conditions.[2] Eczema and other skin rashes can be a sign of an underlying

---

[2] https://www.autismspeaks.org/what-autism/treatment/treatment-associated-medical-conditions

food allergy. Children with these issues should be treated by an immunologist or allergist who is experienced at treating children on the spectrum.

Problems with sleep are also common among children and teens with autism. Many teenagers are on an internal clock that causes them to prefer later bedtimes and wake times, but these sleep problems can be particularly chronic and damaging for children on the spectrum. Lack of sleep or poor-quality sleep can worsen the symptoms of autism in adolescence, including moodiness, distractibility, and aggression. As stated previously, sometimes gastrointestinal disorders can result in sleep disturbances. If you think these issues might be affecting your child, you should consult a gastroenterologist who is familiar with treating kids on the spectrum. Keep in mind that even high-functioning kids with autism can't always reliably communicate what they are feeling, in terms of their emotions and their bodily senses.

In addition, medicines that treat many of the psychiatric issues related to autism, including medications such as SSRIs (selective serotonin reuptake inhibitors, a common form of antidepressant) and stimulant medications to treat the symptoms of ADHD can also affect sleep and sleep patterns. If you have concerns about the effects of these medications on your child, your doctor or psychiatrist can work with you to change the timing or dosage of your child's medication. Some medications affect sleep less if taken in the morning.

If your child struggles to fall asleep or stay asleep, you should consult your doctor to rule out health problems. A doctor can also help your child establish good "sleep hygiene," which refers to setting regular sleep and wake times and habits that induce sleep. These habits include turning off electronics and removing oneself from screens at least an hour before bedtime and moving cell phones and other electronics away from sleep areas, as their glow may make sleep difficult. The hour before bed should be devoted, if possible, to calming activities, such as taking a shower or bath or eating a snack while avoiding stress and work. Taking an herbal supplement called melatonin before bed has also proven helpful to ease sleep for many teens and children with autism. Consult with your doctor before adding melatonin to your child's regimen.

Children with autism are also at an increased risk of epilepsy, as described in Chapter 2. It is estimated that up to 30% of people with autism have epilepsy, compared with 1% to 2% in the neurotypical population. Epilepsy is believed to most commonly co-occur with people who also have intellectual disability. Epilepsy commonly develops when children are in preschool and also during adolescence. Signs can include staring, the involuntary movement of limbs, muscle stiffening, as well as regression (reverting to an earlier developmental stage), aggression, and sleep disturbances. If you have cause to believe that your child is suffering from seizures, you should consult your doctor, who might refer you to a neurologist. Your child may undergo an electroencephalogram (EEG), in which electrodes are placed on the head to monitor brain activity. If your child undergoes this procedure, a social story, with visual cues about what is going to happen to him, can be helpful to prepare him and enable him to be more cooperative with the medical staff.

FINDING THE RIGHT DOCTOR

Although children and teens on the spectrum have additional health care needs that are often unmet, the training for primary care doctors in autism lags behind patients' need for care. Some areas, such as Boston, New Jersey, and Minneapolis, are notable for facilities that offer health care for children and adults with autism. It's rare to find a pediatrician who handles autism, but it is even more rare to find a primary care doctor for adults with autism.

When parents are trying to find the right doctor for their child, whether it's a primary care doctor, a specialist, or a psychiatrist, it's critical to interview potential physicians to make sure they have experience treating people on the spectrum. The doctor working to provide your child with medical care should be knowledgeable about not only the core symptoms of autism but also the common coexisting medical and psychological symptoms that can present themselves as your child ages. The doctor should have an awareness of the progression of autism over the lifetime and help you anticipate and treat changes that occur as your child grows up. Going to the doctor will feel less stressful if your child's physician also understands your and your child's cultural background and other elements that are important in her care, such as religion, race, gender, sexuality, and other concerns.

Here are some questions you may want to ask prospective doctors:

- Have you worked with teenagers or young adults on the autism spectrum before?

- What types of resources and services can you connect me to if my child needs additional help, and are these services covered by insurance?

- What types of parental support do you offer? Are you, for example, available to speak by phone or to meet in between appointments? Do you charge for these sessions?

- What is your philosophy about medications? (Some doctors, for example, prefer patients to have behavioral or psychological interventions before taking medications.)

This list is only an example. You can develop questions that assess whether the doctor is knowledgeable about treating teens and young adults on the autism spectrum and whether he or she will be available to speak with you on a regular basis. In addition, you can ask a bit about his or her treatment plan and philosophy to understand how he or she might work with your child.

Keep in mind that when your child reaches 18, parents and caregivers are cut out of their children's health care decisions. This is true even if children's developmental age lags behind their chronological age. If you are concerned about your child's ability to navigate the health care system and advocate for himself, you should become his legal guardian. This will give you access to your children's health care decisions (there is more information about becoming a legal guardian in Chapter 7).

AUTISM IN THE AFRICAN AMERICAN COMMUNITY

Research such as that by Ruby Gourdine and colleagues has shown that although autism occurs at the same rates among all racial groups, the diagnosis generally occurs later for African American children. As a result, African American children with autism may need treatment that is longer in duration and more intensive. African American children often face limited health care options because of lack of insurance coverage, and African Americans often face racism in medical care. It's important for African Americans to feel that they can trust their child's doctors and to work with them to find treatments and support that they are comfortable with. In addition, it's vital for African American children and teens and other people of color to be included in research studies going forward so the medical community has more information about how autism affects people of different races and backgrounds.

There are some grassroots organizations that support African American families with autistic children. Autism in Black (http://www.autisminblack.com/medical.html) and The Color of Autism (https://www.thecolorofautism.org/programs) offer programs and information for the African American autism community.

HOSPITALIZATIONS

Unfortunately, hospitalizations are more common among children with ASD than among other children. One study by Lisa Croen and colleagues found that children with ASD are 6 times as likely to be hospitalized for psychiatric reasons, including self-injurious behavior and aggression, than other children. Other children on the spectrum are admitted for neurological reasons, such as seizures, or commonly for gastrointestinal or other symptoms. Hospitalization rates for children on the spectrum have been rising in recent years, particularly for teens with psychiatric issues.[3] The rise might in part be accounted for by the lack of community resources to help children and teens with autism, such as respite care. The rise in hospitalizations points to the need for much greater community and school support for spectrum kids to prevent the need for hospitalizations in the first place.

If your child is admitted to the hospital, it is particularly important to let the hospital staff know what soothes your child, as well her or his triggers. The staff also has to be aware of the child's dangerous behaviors. In addition, children with autism in the hospital may need additional support to care for themselves and to take medication. Visual schedules or reward systems can be helpful in assisting patients with taking medication and undergoing medical procedures. Hospital staff can provide patients with sensory tools, weighted blankets, and other items that soothe their sensory system.

STATE HEALTH CARE RULES

States vary with regard to how health care costs related to autism are covered. At the time of publication, Massachusetts had one of the most generous provisions of benefits, as laws state that health care companies cannot set an annual or lifetime limit or caps on the cost of autism-related services that is less than the limit for physical conditions and cannot limit visits to a provider of autism services. States that do not set limits on autism coverage include California, Indiana, and Minnesota. New Jersey also has generous benefits related to health care for autism. Other states have limits, though generous ones, such

---

[3] https://www.ncbi.nlm.nih.gov/pubmed/17975720

as Pennsylvania and New York. Several states set age limits, 21 or 16 years, for the provision of autism services. Some states have laws providing for some services, such as ABA, but have few providers and very long waiting lists. In addition, in some states, ABA providers do not accept Medicaid.

Some families decide to move to another state to access better autism-related services. Although that decision is dependent on many factors, the biggest factor for many families is whether the services provided will allow their children to make gains. Families weigh the cost of living with the availability of services when considering a move, and anecdotally, many have chosen Pennsylvania (particularly near Pittsburgh) as a place with a great availability of services and a lower cost of living.

A 2011 survey by Autism Speaks identified the greater metropolitan areas of New York, Los Angeles, Chicago, Cleveland, Philadelphia, and Boston as the best places for people with autism to live. Northern New Jersey, Seattle, Minneapolis/St. Paul, and Milwaukee were also among the top 10 places to live with autism, and the lowest-ranked states included Texas, Virginia, Tennessee, Ohio, Florida, Michigan, and California. The criteria that went into the rankings included educational and other services, clinical/medical care, and recreational activities. Those in the lowest ranking states cited the long distances they had to travel to access services and the lack of medical and recreational activities. People in all areas of the country cited a lack of available respite care.

The availability of ASD-related services in rural areas is a particular problem, and studies have shown that families in rural areas face difficulties accessing care for autism diagnosis and treatment. If you live in a rural area and have a lack of autism-related services, you may have access to a telehealth program such as ECHO (Extension for Community Health Outcomes). The ECHO program uses videoconferencing to provide help from specialists at cutting-edge health care providers such as the University of Missouri Thompson Center for Autism and Neurodevelopmental Disorders, Vanderbilt University, the University of Rochester, and the Lurie Center for Autism in the Boston area with local health care providers in rural and underserved areas. This is only one example of a telehealth program that is enabling families to receive care from autism specialists.

DENTAL CARE

Dental care can be difficult for children with autism, and this problem persists into adolescence. The sensory and taste issues associated with autism can make it difficult for children on the spectrum to brush their teeth well. Some teens with autism continue to struggle with keeping their teeth clean, and parents may need to continue to help their teens brush well by giving them a timer to make sure they are brushing long enough and by providing them with visual steps about how to brush their teeth. If your child works with an ABA therapist, that person can be helpful in moving your child toward independence in dental care.

Autism Speaks has provided resources for helping children on the spectrum prepare for dental visits and helping dental professionals prepare to work with patients on the spectrum.[4] One tip is to call the dentist's office in advance to let them know more about your child. You may also want to request appointment times when there aren't likely to be too many other patients in the office.

BRACES AND ORTHODONTIA

Braces and orthodontia may pose particular problems for preteens and teens on the spectrum. It certainly helps for kids to get advance information about what is going to happen during a visit to the orthodontist. This information could come

[4] https://www.autismspeaks.org/sites/default/files/documents/dentalguide.pdf

in the form of a social story. Make sure the orthodontists who work with your teen are aware of her sensory issues and any increased sensitivity to dental discomfort, as well as your child's ability to communicate and to describe her discomfort.

You may decide that it's not necessary for your spectrum teen to have straight teeth. Parents sometimes make this choice because they know that their children will struggle with the sensory and other demands of wearing braces and retainers. In addition, the cost of orthodontia is high and may not be possible for families with high out-of-pocket expenses related to health care, ABA services, and psychiatric services, so families may decide that they can't afford the cost of braces. If you make this choice for your child, feel confident that you are providing him with what he most needs at this time and that straight teeth, although important for some families, may not be his first concern.

REFLECTIONS ON PARENTING

It can be overwhelming to realize that at each step of your child's development, you may need to find specialized medical practitioners who understand your child's needs and who have the necessary skills to weigh the different physical, psychological, and other variables in his or her treatment. Without a doubt, this places added burden on you as a parent; however, it is also an opportunity to make sure that your child is in the right hands, medically speaking.

You may at first feel reluctant to ask so many questions before you start working with a professional, but at this stage of your child's development, you likely already know what types of people you and your child will work well with. There are more and more professionals who are trained to work with people on the spectrum, and you and your child will likely benefit more from working with people who have this type of knowledge and who are willing to give you and your child the additional time you need. For example, a doctor who rushes you out of the office and who does not take the time to explain procedures—using words or social stories—to your child will likely not be a good fit. Your doctors should not regard these types of accommodations as excessive but as part of good practice for teens and young adults on the spectrum and their families.

PARENTING STRATEGIES

- Find medical and therapeutic care for your child from professionals who are knowledgeable about and experienced in treating children and teens with ASD.

- Develop a series of questions to ask potential doctors before you start working with them.

- If your child is hospitalized, work with the staff to explain your child's behaviors and what soothes her.

- Learn what your state provides in terms of autism-related services. Some states require employers to cover ABA services, whereas others do not or have caps or age limits.

- Areas of the country also vary with regard to the availability of medical and behavioral professionals. Consider telehealth alternatives if you live in a remote area.

- Be aware of the ways in which health and psychiatric issues associated with autism can affect the core symptoms of autism. Get treatment for your child if he has gastrointestinal issues or sleep problems, for example.

- If your child is visiting the doctor or needs to be hospitalized, you can ease the process by providing social stories or videos in advance and letting the relevant staff know about your child's needs and sensitivities. Use Autism Speaks and other websites to find relevant social stories to help your child prepare for medical and dental visits.

- Prepare your child for dental or orthodontic procedures in advance, and prepare the staff members to help your child.

6

Coaching Your Child About Sex, Safety, and Self-Care

Felix was a friendly 11-year-old kid who liked to greet everyone he met at the local park. One day, he encountered a 15-year-old boy who seemed annoyed by Felix. When Felix kept trying to engage the older boy in a basketball game, the boy grabbed Felix's private parts and threatened him. Felix suffered trauma as a result of this incident and would not go to the park again.

Julian was a handsome 16-year-old boy with high-functioning autism who projected more sophistication than he really had. When a girl sent him an Instagram photo of her nude body, he forwarded it to other students in his grade, thinking it was kind of a joke. He was suspended from school for sexual harassment as a result.

When Grace first got her period, she found that she didn't know how to manage carrying sanitary pads to school and didn't know how to bring them with her to the bathroom. She needed the help of some of her aides to figure out how and when to change her pads regularly, and she and her aides came up with a schedule so that she could take care of herself on her own.

DATING AND SEX

There is no more fraught topic for parents with spectrum kids than dating and sex. Kids on the spectrum struggle to understand complex, nuanced social situations—just the kinds of situations that dating and sex place them into. As many people in our society rightfully question traditional modes of male–female interaction, in many ways the dating situation has become more loaded and complex than ever before. On the other hand, there are some clear rules that can help teens with autism.

You should speak with your teen about dating and sex long before they are actually dating. Because children on the spectrum may struggle with social abstractions, it's best to keep the matter practical and as straightforward as possible. Teens can become interested in dating and sex even if they seem less mature than their chronological age. One caregiver was surprised when the 17-year-old boy she was watching over the summer suddenly started kissing a girl, who also had autism, as the caregiver was driving them home. The boy had made remarkable gains after not being able to speak at age 6, but he still sometimes struggled with communication and was not at the level of maturity of a typically developing 12-year-old, not to mention a 17-year-old. Nonetheless, he seemed interested in dating, or at least in having physical relationships.

Social stories can be very helpful in training teens on the spectrum to understand how to ask someone out and what to expect on a date. They can also learn about different stages of intimacy, including holding hands, kissing, hugging, and sex. They need to be explicitly told about asking for and giving verbal consent to different stages of intimacy through the use of social stories, video modeling, and/or role playing. Teens also need to understand that at times, dating has no rules. For example, they may not understand who is more likely and less likely to accept their invitation to go out and may need to learn how to get to know someone before asking that person out on a date.

The Internet and social media complicate all of these issues, and teens need explicit rules about what to post and not to post online (as do typically developing teens). Spectrum teens tend to be good rule followers, but they may not understand more complicated and nuanced rules such as not forwarding the insulting or harassing e-mails or posts.

SEXUAL ABUSE

It can be quite scary for parents to learn that people with developmental disabilities (not just autism) are sexually abused at twice the rate of the general population, according to research by Meredyth Edelson. Spectrum kids' relative weakness in interpreting and understanding the motivations and emotions of other people makes them particularly vulnerable to sexual abuse. This is particularly true of malicious and deceptive behavior. Perpetrators may also target nonverbal children, as they expect that their victims can't inform on them.

It is important for parents to realize that even verbal children will not always tell caregivers about incidents of sexual harassment or abuse because of communication issues. For example, Felix, who suffered trauma after an older boy grabbed his genitals in a park, did not tell anyone about this incident because he was afraid he'd get in trouble and he didn't know how to tell his parents what happened (typically developing teens can also be reluctant to tell their parents about abuse out of fear that they will be in trouble).

It's not my purpose to cause undue stress, but I do always advise parents to be attentive to changes in their child's behavior, including worsening aggression, self-injurious behaviors, or sexualized behaviors. Caregivers should not assume that these behaviors are indicative only of autism, as changes in behavior can indicate that a child has been abused. For example, Felix in the previous anecdote became much more aggressive after he was abused, and he also began to use words that he had never used before and to ask people whether he could expose his genitals or put them on other people. His parents were only able to get the story of what had happened to him by promising him he wasn't in trouble.

When they asked him why he hadn't told them what happened, Felix explained, "I didn't have time the next day before the school bus came in the morning." Felix's response indicates that many spectrum kids, even those considered "high functioning" in medical parlance, may not realize that communicating sexual abuse is important. In addition, spectrum kids tend to interpret questions very literally, so when his parents repeatedly asked if an adult had done something scary to him or touched him inappropriately before they finally discovered what had happened, Felix responded no. He later explained that he had answered that way because a teenager had touched him, not an adult.

Parents have to let their children know in advance, using social stories, that any kind of unwanted sexual contact is wrong. In addition, high-functioning children with autism must be informed about how to interpret the signs of others when they are signaling that they do not want sexual contact to avoid their perpetration of sexual abuse.

BIRTH CONTROL

The American Academy of Pediatrics has recommended that a conversation about birth control and sexuality be part of the routine care of teens and young adults with disabilities, including autism. People on the spectrum are often regarded as asexual or not likely to engage in sexual behavior, but this is not the case. Doctors should let their patients on the spectrum know about birth control options in the same way they would advise other teens (of all genders, including transgender people) about these options. Some girls and women on the spectrum may require birth control options to control menstruation if they are on different types of medication or struggle with hygiene issues. Your doctor is the best person to consult about these options, and you can follow up with your doctor about your teen's visit in which sexuality and birth control were discussed.

PERSONAL HYGIENE

Sensory issues and weakness in social understanding can make it hard for kids on the spectrum to understand proper hygiene and to follow it. Your teen may struggle when having his hair or nails cut, and sensory issues can complicate bathing and shaving. Though other typically developing kids can become more aware of the need for socially appropriate grooming as they age, kids on the spectrum may not always develop this awareness on their own.

As with all autism-related skills, parents can help their kids by breaking down the steps involved in activities such as taking a shower, brushing one's teeth, applying deodorant, brushing one's hair, and shaving. Laminated visual aids and lists can be posted in the bathroom so that preteens and teens remember everything that they need to do. The other adults who work with your child, including therapists, ABA (applied behavior analysis) therapists, teachers, or others, can also help reinforce the routines.

When buying hygiene products for your child, be aware of the sensory demands of each aspect of grooming. For example, some spectrum children and teens dislike heavy scents and may need to pick out the scents they like or use unscented products. Teens may need to use hair-removing creams or electric razors rather than razor blades for safety and sensory reasons. Using social stories can help kids understand the importance of proper hygiene, and they might also respond well to video modeling. You can film someone preparing for the day in the morning and show each step, such as the person applying deodorant with multiple swipes across the armpit, so that your child understands the steps involved in getting ready.

Parents can also consult a book called *Hygiene and Related Behaviors for Children and Adolescents with Autism Spectrum and Related Disorders: A Fun Curriculum with a Focus on Social Understanding* by Kelly J. Mahler. This guide breaks down activities that are involved in hygiene and also provides a CD and printable worksheets. The activities are intended to be fun, and they can also be carried out by teachers and related professionals working with children and adolescents with autism.

MENSTRUATION

Menstruation can be a very difficult issue for parents and girls on the spectrum. Although the average age of the onset of menstruation is 12, many girls start menstruating younger, and parents and their daughters need to prepare in advance for the changes that menstruation bring. Girls with autism have more abnormal hormonal changes in general, and these issues can complicate their menstrual periods and result in cramps, irregular periods, or acne. Menstruation may make them more aggressive or obsessive and may result in increased seizure activity or depression.[1] Parents should monitor their daughters for these changes and seek help from their doctors if needed.

Carrying out the necessary self-care to deal with having their periods can also be difficult for girls on the spectrum, and having to wear tampons or pads can cause them to have sensory issues or worsen their sensory issues. Girls on the spectrum need help in keeping track of their periods and anticipating when their period might arrive. They also need help to pack and carry tampons, pads, and a change of clothing. Pads might be easier for girls with autism to handle than tampons if pads are able to absorb the flow.

Breaking down the steps involved in how they can practice self-care can help, and they may need repetition and social stories to reinforce the information. They may need schedules set up, perhaps with a reminder set on their phone or computer, about when to change their pads. The idea is

---

[1] https://www.scientificamerican.com/article/autism-it-s-different-in-girls/ and https://www.epilepsy.com/learn/triggers-seizures/menstruation

to eventually enable your daughter to carry out these tasks on her own, though it may take some support before she is ready to do so.

SLEEP

Sleep can be problematic for kids of any age on the spectrum. As discussed in Chapter 5, sleep disturbances can be caused or worsened by health and psychological issues that are common to people on the spectrum, including gastrointestinal disorders or issues such as depression and anxiety. In general, children who are undergoing transitions tend to show a more pronounced degree of sleep problems. Having insufficient sleep can worsen the core symptoms of autism, including aggression, irritability, and distractibility. Medications often given to children and teens for autism, including SSRIs (selective serotonin reuptake inhibitors, a common form of antidepressant), can also affect sleep, so it's worthwhile to work with your doctor on the timing of these medications to optimize daytime wakefulness and nighttime sleep.

Routines that help younger children with sleep issues can also help teens. Teens should set a regular time for bed, and they can follow visual schedules to prepare for sleeping. The bedtime routine can include activities that your child finds relaxing, including reading or listening to music. Spectrum kids need to feel comfortable in their clothing and bed to sleep well, and many do well with weighted blankets to soothe their senses. Turning off electronics an hour before bedtime aids sleep, as does storing charging electronics (whose glow can keep people awake) far from sleep areas. People who exercise for more than 30 minutes a day find it easier to sleep, and having a light meal and avoiding caffeine before bed can also help. Teens tend to go to sleep later and wake up later than younger kids, but they still need about 9 hours of sleep per night. Going to bed too late can result in insufficient sleep. If your teen struggles with sleep, consult with your doctor about taking a supplement called melatonin, which aids people with the sleep–wake cycle.

EXERCISE

Exercise has been shown to be of vital importance to people with autism. Studies by Reed Elliott and colleagues have found that aerobic exercise reduces stereotypical and maladaptive behaviors among people with autism. Other studies (such as that by Spanish psychologist Domingo Antonio García Villamisar and colleagues) have demonstrated that leisure programs in general, which include exercise, crafts, and other activities, significantly reduced the stress level of young adults with autism and increased their life satisfaction. Exercise has been shown to lower depression, hyperactivity, and destructiveness. There are also cognitive benefits, such as improved memory. Sufficient exercise is also important to regulate sleep.

Everyone can benefit from exercise, but it's particularly critical for children and teens on the spectrum. Though they may not always have access to structured sports activities, they often enjoy activities that stimulate their sensory systems, such as jumping on a trampoline or swimming. Some kids on the spectrum enjoy sports that don't involve a high level of social cooperation, such as running or track. Coaches and instructors might have to break down the activities involved in exercise and adapt these activities as needed to account for children's and teen's fine and gross motor skills. Resistance bands and exercise balls can be helpful for children to develop strength and skills. In some areas of the country, there are physical trainers who specialize in working with children with autism. Some of these trainers are also trained in ABA, and they use many of its principles, such as rewards and reinforcement and some element of personal choice, in structuring physical activities.

Although many parents prioritize other activities, such as language or behavioral training, above physical training, exercise has the potential to pay many dividends that can help children with autism in other areas. Teenagers with autism who do not have physical outlets can become more aggressive and dysregulated, and providing them with physical fitness routines can help them establish healthy patterns for adulthood.

DRUGS AND ALCOHOL

It was generally assumed in the past that people with autism did not have drug and alcohol disorders. However, a recent Swedish study by Agnieszka Butwicka and colleagues published in the *Journal of Autism and Developmental Disorders* showed that adults with autism had twice the risk of others to develop substance-abuse disorders, and this rate was even higher for people with autism spectrum disorder (ASD) *and* attention-deficit/hyperactivity disorder (ADHD). Previous studies might have been skewed toward people with more severe forms of ASD, as the diagnosis had not expanded to include people without intellectual disability. Addiction is rarer in people with more severe forms of ASD than in those with more moderate forms of ASD. Another study carried out by the Washington University School of Medicine found that people with autistic traits (though not necessarily a diagnosis of autism) were not more likely to binge drink, but they were more likely to develop alcohol problems if they began to drink. People in the study with traits related to autism and ADHD were also more likely to abuse marijuana. The authors speculated that people with autistic traits might favor drinking alone, as opposed to social drinking, and this practice might increase their risk for developing alcohol problems.

One reason that some teens on the spectrum might turn to drug and alcohol use is to alleviate anxiety, particularly social anxiety. In addition, many people on the spectrum have obsessive-compulsive disorder, and their compulsions and impulsive behavior can also drive them to use drugs and alcohol. Some face jarring sensory issues, and others use drugs and alcohol to find the pleasure that many people derive from social interactions.

Parents should be aware that just because their teen doesn't "party" or hang out with peers in typical ways, he or she might still be at risk for developing drug and alcohol problems. Many spectrum teens may be driven to reduce their anxiety through drinking or smoking marijuana. If people with autism need drug or alcohol treatment, they may not benefit from traditional group treatment approaches in which they have to be sensitive and responsive to others' emotions and treatments. Instead, they might benefit more from cognitive behavioral therapy and individual approaches to treatment.

It should be noted that researchers are just beginning to learn more about autism and alcohol and drug dependence. The new research into this area is helping to refine and develop prevention and treatment plans for people with autism. By treating the psychiatric issues that drive alcohol and drug addiction with therapy and medications, you can help your teen stay away from addictive substances. If you haven't done so already, start speaking with your child about drugs and alcohol, even if he is a few years away from being a teen.

STRESS AND SENSORY MANAGEMENT

Teaching your child or teen techniques to handle stress is a critical skill to help them through the turbulence of adolescence and to prepare them to face the stress of the adult world. Your child, with your help, can begin to monitor his body for signs of stress, such as rapid or shallow breathing, sweating, tight muscles, or clenched hands, among other signs. He can be cued to start deep breathing or practicing muscle relaxation techniques to get through these episodes. Sometimes people on the spectrum need numbers to calibrate how they are feeling (for example, 1 is *calm*, building up to 4, which is *explosive*). They can begin to identify where they are on an escalation of emotions and take a break before their stress level reaches the highest point.

Your child should also identify where he can go if he feels overwhelmed, either by emotional stress or sensory overload. At home, space permitting, you can use a basement or other space to create a calm area with helpful sensory input such as a bean bag chair. In school, there should be a safe area, such as part of a nurse's office, where your child can go to de-stress. If this type of area does not exist, speak to your child's school administration about creating one.

Mindfulness has been shown to be effective in reducing stress and anxiety and can result in better sleep and quality of life. (Mindfulness can also be critical in helping the parents of children with ASD manage stress; see Chapter 8 for more information.) Mindfulness enables the person, with practice over time, to have some distance and perspective on her immediate, emotional response to stress and to exercise some control over her response. Research has shown that practicing mindfulness techniques over time helps lead to a decreased connection between the amygdala, the part of the brain involved in processing emotions, and other sections of the brain. This reduces the overreactive tendencies of the amygdala. Mindfulness techniques must be taught in the same way other behaviors are taught—with each step broken down and practiced over time when the child or teen is calm and receptive.

One form of mindfulness that may be useful (but that has not been tested empirically) involves building on the synesthesia that is very common among people with autism. Synesthesia is a condition in which one sense is automatically related to another sense; in one common form of synesthesia, letters and numbers are associated with specific colors. For example, people with synesthesia may always see a "2" or a "B" as pink. Teens and young adults with synesthesia (or just with associations between colors and moods) can be taught to see moods and emotions as colors. For example, if they associate red with anger, they can be taught to breathe out red (in other words, to imagine red clouds of anger escaping from their mouths) and to breathe in a color that they associate with peacefulness and tranquility, such as blue or purple. Using strategies that build on synesthesia may help them understand how to breathe out anger and stress and how to breathe in calmness and relaxation when practicing mindfulness techniques.

EATING AND SENSORY ISSUES

As children with autism move through their adolescent years, they may gain a great deal of weight and develop unhealthy eating habits. They may not always have reliable ways to exercise, and some of the medications that treat the symptoms of autism can cause weight gain. In addition, sensory issues and selectivity about food can make it difficult for them to eat a balanced diet. And, as mentioned earlier, behavioral reward systems can involve allowing kids to eat a lot of junk food for meeting target goals. Gaining excess weight can result in more anxiety, worse sleep patterns, and future health issues.

Dietitians, behavioral therapists, and occupational therapists can help preteens and teens develop better eating habits; experts suggest that children on the spectrum with eating issues can benefit from a multidisciplinary team to help them develop healthier eating habits that work around their sensory issues. (In addition, if your child works with an ABA therapist, that person can be encouraged to reward your child with things such as shooting baskets or jumping on a trampoline rather than with junk food.) Occupational therapists can help pinpoint your child's food issues and help her expand her diet by introducing new, healthier foods that your child might like. For example, although your child may react to the consistency of some fruits, perhaps she would be able to stomach a smoothie or have fruit mixed in with yogurt. Children and teens on the spectrum tend to be resistant to change, so introduce food changes one at a time to find out what your child is willing to eat and hopefully to make her diet healthier and more varied.

The website Cooking With Autism (https://www.cooking withautism.com) is a great resource to help your child learn how to cook. This organization offers cooking classes tailored to people with autism and Asperger's syndrome and publishes a book called *Coach in the Kitchen* with recipes tested to work well for chefs with gross or fine motor issues, food sensitivities, sensory issues, and problems following multistep directions.

EATING DISORDERS IN AUTISM

Research in the past 15 years indicates a connection between eating disorders and ASD. Elisabet Wentz and colleagues found that among the female patients with eating disorders in the study, 23% had ASD. In fact, because many girls with Asperger's—as high-functioning autism used to be known in the medical literature and is sometimes still popularly known—are not diagnosed with autism (perhaps in part because of a misunderstanding of how autism can manifest itself in girls and women), they are often initially referred to psychiatric care for eating disorders. For that reason, some experts refer to eating disorders as the "female Asperger's."[2]

People with ASD and anorexia often have similar cognitive profiles; for example, people who go on to develop anorexia can have problems relating to others and show very rigid behaviors. They also tend to have a pointillist perspective that prevents them from seeing the bigger picture. In addition, they are not always sensitive to, or aware of, the ways in which their disordered eating patterns affect others.

---

[2] https://spectrumnews.org/features/deep-dive/the-invisible-link-between-autism-and-anorexia/

It can be difficult for girls on the spectrum who have eating disorders to receive treatment, as not many clinicians are, at this point, trained in both fields. In addition, eating disorders and/or compulsive exercising may be a means of trying to keep anxiety at bay and to create order in a disordered world. In this sense, eating disorders, although dangerous and harmful, may be serving a purpose for girls with ASD (boys and men can also present with eating and exercise disorders). People with ASD may not feel comfortable receiving group therapeutic treatment for eating disorders and may need a more individualized approach. In addition, the desire of people with ASD for routines may make it difficult to create successful interventions in their eating issues as these interventions involve changing routines and established practices, and these issues may be compounded by sensory sensitivities. If your child is having eating-related problems, realize that they are more common among people with ASD than was once commonly thought.

REFLECTIONS ON PARENTING

When you try to teach your child skills related to sexuality, dating, and self-care, it is normal to feel afraid and even defensive. At best, your child might follow the important rules for online sharing, even while she does not follow other, less vital rules, such as applying deodorant or taking a shower regularly, leading her to smell bad in front of others. You may have to struggle with your own embarrassment about these issues until your child develops her own grooming skills. At worst, your child may run into sexual misunderstandings that have legal, medical, and other complications. Tackling these issues can be complicated.

Your child may need more time than her peers to practice the skills necessary to develop better hygiene and sexual health practices, and to make healthy decisions about dating. For each step, provide social stories if necessary and recognize that with some help, your teen or young adult child can get there. It's natural to wish that your child was still young or to be frustrated about her slow progress toward taking care of herself, but helping her toward greater independence in these areas is essential.

PARENTING STRATEGIES

- Realize that although your child's maturation might be below his chronological age, he might still be interested in dating and sex and may need explicit training in these areas to be safe.

- Be aware of your child's vulnerability to sexual abuse. Watch his or her behaviors for any changes that could indicate abuse.

- You and the professionals who work with your child can help her develop skills related to dating and grooming in the same way she works on other skills—by breaking them down into steps, using visual aids, and assisting them with repetition.

- Develop checklists and visual aids that help your child work toward independence in self-care and in grooming. Post these lists in the bathroom so that your child can follow them on her own.

- Try to turn off screens and electronics at least an hour before bedtime, and prepare a light snack for your child to help him sleep. You can also speak with your child's doctor about the timing of medications and about taking a melatonin supplement.

- Help your teen or young adult develop exercise and mindfulness habits that are tailored to his abilities and that help him with stress reduction.

- Consult dietitians and occupational and behavioral therapists to slowly transition your child to a healthier diet that also accommodates her sensory needs.

7

Adulthood and Beyond

Jimena had a lot to offer prospective employers. Having graduated with a degree in biochemistry, she had good academic credentials and excellent personal qualities, such as honesty, integrity, punctuality, and loyalty. However, she was repeatedly rejected after being interviewed because she found it difficult to speak about her qualifications and skills while being grilled by prospective employers.

When Noah was a senior in high school, his guidance counselor suggested that he enroll in a dual-enrollment program at his local community college, which had a program for students on the spectrum. That way, he could continue to receive services, such as counseling and life skills, from his high school while dipping his toe into college waters and becoming more independent.

When Bill turned 17, he started to think about his own goals. He decided that he enjoyed visiting the local greenhouse and had already classified each type of flower and tree there. He was part of the individualized education program (IEP) process that helped him find an internship at a greenhouse and that established which goals he would work on in the coming year, including shopping for groceries, doing his own laundry, and learning to drive.

NEW STUDIES ABOUT ADULTHOOD WITH AUTISM SPECTRUM DISORDER

Research into autism has accelerated in recent years, and the first wave of people with autism spectrum disorder (ASD) who have been followed since childhood is now reaching adulthood. These longitudinal studies are giving us a much clearer picture of the way autism affects people over the lifetime. For example, a study in 2016 by Inge-Marie Eigsti referenced in Chapter 2 discovered that many young adults who had been diagnosed with ASD as young children no longer met criteria for the diagnosis. Some continued to display softer signs of the disorder, such as problems with social communication or shifting their attention, or attention-deficit/hyperactivity disorder (ADHD). In other words, some people with autism experience an improvement in the core symptoms of autism as they age into young adulthood. This chapter presents the most current research and strategies about how spectrum teens and their parents and caregivers can navigate the teens' transition to young adulthood.

Julie Lounds Taylor, a professor at Vanderbilt University, and Paul Shattuck at Drexel University have done cutting-edge research into the transition to adulthood for people with autism. Shattuck documented the so-called "cliff" that young adults fall off of after graduating from high school, as they receive few medical, mental health, or other services. Researchers believe that rather than trying to make people with autism seem neurotypical, society should instead provide vocational, housing, and other support to young adults with autism. Such supports would be worth the investment, as data have shown that these adults can contribute to the workplace if they are given a chance to do so.

These recent studies inform our understanding of the ways in which autism continues to affect people as they age. In addition, the field is only beginning to benefit from longitudinal studies that track people with autism over time, particularly people who benefited from empirically validated interventions as children.

Early adulthood can also be a time of progress, as cognitive development in the prefrontal cortex area of the brain can help curb some of the symptoms of ADHD, which include hyperactivity, impulsivity, and inattentiveness. As many people with ASD also struggle with ADHD, they can show improvement in tasks requiring attention, organization, flexibility, and planning as they get older. Their emotional or aggressive responses may taper, and they may show greater logic and emotional self-control.

For many young adults with high-functioning autism, however, their seemingly functional veneer can hide vulnerabilities and autistic symptoms, and they can still use compensatory strategies. The book *Aquamarine Blue: Personal Stories of College Students with Autism* by Dawn Prince-Hughes (2002) provides insights into what it's like to be a young adult with high-functioning autism (or what was formerly called Asperger's syndrome) in the college setting. For example, one of the writers speaks about how she could only eat one food at a time because of sensory issues. She was nearly sent to an inpatient program for what the school administration diagnosed as anorexia. When her actual difficulties were uncovered, she was eventually permitted to eat in the cafeteria before other students ate, to avoid the noise and visual chaos. Another student writes about how he felt forced to give up the "stimming behaviors" that brought him comfort so that he could fit into the adult world.

Therefore, although autism symptoms may lessen into adulthood, young adults with ASD can still struggle with sensory issues, social isolation, and emotional dysregulation, though they may also have learned to develop coping strategies over time. For example, they might have learned how to ask questions of professors and how to let their employers know that they need to work from home to avoid the noise and fluorescent lights of the office. They can also work in an area of skill—whether it's computers, science, writing, math, painting, design, or something else—that compels their attention and caters to their strengths.

TRANSITION PLANNING

By federal law (the Individuals With Disabilities Education Act, or IDEA), schools must start planning for students with autism to make a transition to college, the workforce, or independent living starting when the students are 16. Some states provide for this transition starting at age 14, which allows more preparation time for parents and students. This planning must be part of a student's IEP (individualized education program), and the program must be based on the child's needs and strengths and include not only academic instruction but also related services; community experiences; and goals related to employment, college, and functional daily living skills.

As your child gets older, it can be very helpful and productive for him to become part of the IEP process, particularly around issues of the transition beyond school. If your child can participate in setting some of his own goals and then progress toward writing his goals on his own, it will help his own sense of being in control over his future and will increase his investment in fulfilling his goals.

FINDING A COLLEGE PROGRAM

There are different types of college programs for students on the spectrum. Some students attend mainstream colleges and receive individual support, including tutoring or coaching that works with their academic and social needs. They are responsible for determining the kinds of support they need, and they may also use campus resources such as learning specialists, therapists, or writing center or subject-matter tutors. In these types of programs, there is no formal program for students with autism, and students must feel comfortable advocating for their needs and meeting with professors, learning specialists, tutors, and others and asking for the help they require.

In a hybrid model, students attend some classes with mainstream students but might also attend classes that help them with skills and with the transition to college. In a separate model, students with autism attend classes only with other students with autism (or perhaps with students with other disabilities), and they interact with other students by taking part in on-campus activities.

Community colleges also offer some great remedial programs for students with autism; one network that offers these types of programs is the Community College Consortium for Autism and Intellectual Disabilities. These programs may offer the assistance of professors trained to work with college students with autism, and they might also offer job training and social programs for students on the spectrum. The facilitation of social activities for students on the spectrum can be critical, as many young adults with autism are not able to arrive on a new campus and make these social connections on their own.

Services provided through IDEA are not available when a child leaves school (or turns 21), but dual-enrollment programs allow teens to enroll in college while still getting IDEA-funded services. When a student makes the transition to college, he or she is responsible for asking for accommodations under Section 504 of the Rehabilitation Act. This means that the student must present the college with documentation establishing his disability and need for accommodations and must work with the college to request and arrange these accommodations.

When you are working with your child and your high school guidance counselor to find a college that is the right fit for your child, think about the following types of issues/questions:

- How comfortable will my child be asking for help and accommodations?

- How much academic support will my child need, not only for class-based material but also in taking tests, writing papers, planning a schedule, and meeting with professors?

- How much social support will my child need? Can she make friends on her own, or will she need a more structured social program?

- What are the counseling services at the colleges like? Will my child use these services?

- Are there special classes or programs that can help my child make the transition to college or that can help him register for appropriate classes?

- Are there classes or programs that help prepare my child for the workforce or that provide internship opportunities?

If you feel that your child still needs a high level of support but is able to handle college-level work (and you have the resources), I recommend allowing them to attend a supportive college away from home. Many parents try to be the bridge that makes college work for their children by allowing them to continue to live at home when they attend school or by doing a significant portion of the classwork and advocacy work for them. One father I met even wrote his son's papers until his son failed out of college junior year. This is not a healthy setup for you or your child. Think about how college students tend to procrastinate. This situation, in addition to stunting your child's emotional and academic growth, puts you in the position of having to write papers until the wee hours of the night. It's also ethically dishonest. Think College (https://thinkcollege.net) can help you find options for students with intellectual disability.

Instead of pushing your child to attend a more prestigious or less supportive school, take stock of where he or she is by senior year of high school. For example, consider whether your child can do the following on his or her own:

- Speak to teachers.

- Ask for needed accommodations, such as breaks or extra time for tests.

- Write papers.

- Take notes in class.

- Make doctor's appointments.

- Get out of bed.

- Make friends and social connections.

In addition, assess your child's ability to carry out life skills, including the following:

- Making a budget and sticking to it and using money.

- Being able to use public transportation and walk places safely. Walking safely requires people to have a developed "theory of mind" (the ability to comprehend others' points of view) because pedestrians have to assess whether motorists are going to stop for them and sometimes have to make eye contact with motorists to make this determination.

- Doing laundry, wearing appropriate clothing, and maintaining proper hygiene.

- Preparing simple meals.

If your child can't do these things on his own, his chances to succeed in a mainstream school aren't good. There are many parents who try to prop their kids up in high school by doing the work for them. This refers not only to the academic work but also to the vital work of being a student—asking teachers questions, figuring out how to study, and determining how one works best. This is understandable. We all want our kids to succeed. However, when a child goes to a college and has these props taken away from him, he will likely flounder and feel worse about himself when he has to take time off from school or drop out completely. It's far better to start with more support, such as at a community college that's set up for students with autism or another supportive program, and have trained professionals work to prepare your child to enter a less restrictive college in 2 years or prepare him to enter the workforce.

In Chapter 3, I mentioned Paul Shattuck and colleagues' research about the two critical skills that students with autism must possess to prepare for independence: identity formation and self-efficacy. All young adults go through the process of identity formation, which is the process of developing and refining one's identity based on race, gender, ethnic background, and disability identity. Self-efficacy is the belief that one can be successful at what one does. Both components must be in place for a student to successfully advocate for herself. She must know what her needs are, and she must believe that she can be successful. It's not necessary for students to refer to or think about having autism as a disability. If a student has not yet developed these components by college, it's essential for her to enroll in the type of program that will help her develop these skills.

SEARCHING FOR A JOB

A report by the A. J. Drexel Autism Center found that only 58% of young adults with autism had worked for pay during the first 8 years out of high school. This rate is much lower than that of young adults with learning issues. In addition, those young adults who worked tended to receive low wages. One of the authors of the study, Paul Shattuck, believes that part of the issue is that the jobs being created in the United States tend to focus on the provision of services, and these jobs require interpersonal skills. The jobs in automation, such as working on assembly lines, that were available in the past did not require this set of skills.

Young adults with autism often need support to determine their interests, write resumes, conduct job searches, and go on interviews. They may need support in figuring out how their skills can be transferred to a job. In addition, they do not tend to have the type of developed social networks of typical twentysomethings, and social networks are an important part of conducting informational interviews and of finding a job. In addition, young adults with autism may not know how to speak about their skills or match their skills to that of the employer. This is in spite of their considerable skills in certain areas.

Nonprofit organizations have sprung up in many communities to help young adults with autism with the "soft skills" they need to find work. In addition, some enlightened employers, such as Microsoft, have changed the interview process for potential hires so that candidates do not have to be grilled by interviewers and can instead be observed working. This is likely a more reliable way to assess most candidates, and it allows people on the spectrum to avoid a potentially difficult interview. Some states, such as Massachusetts, have also allowed people with autism to receive job training from the Department of Developmental Services (which formerly restricted these services to people with lower IQs).

When people with autism fill jobs, they tend to have qualities that make them stellar employees, including loyalty, punctuality, and honesty. Once they get over the initial hurdle of getting a job, employees with autism may also need very specific job training, and their managers might need to break down complicated instructions and make instructions explicit. Although employment for adults on the spectrum still lags behind where it should be, there is increasing interest among employers in hiring and retaining workers with ASD, and we hope and expect that employment and job training programs for young adults on the spectrum will increase in the coming years as more and more spectrum kids reach adulthood.

LEGAL GUARDIANSHIP

Parents who need to continue to make health care and financial decisions for their children who are over 18 need to become the legal guardians of their young adult children. The first step is usually to consult with an attorney about setting up a will (or trust) that includes a special needs trust for your child to safeguard his or her receipt of government benefits such as SSI (Supplemental Security Income) and Medicaid, to ensure the management of inherited assets, and to set up the care of your child. A special needs trust allows you to set aside money for your child in addition to government benefits. Your lawyer can advise you about the next steps, which often involve a legal hearing before a judge.

One benefit of setting up a legal guardianship is that in most states, adults over the age of 18 are assumed to be able to make their own health care decisions. In many states, you will not be able to make health care decisions for your child over 18 if he is admitted to a hospital, for example, without being a legal guardian (although some states have health care rules that will allow parents to make decisions without going through the legal guardianship procedure).

If your child has a legal guardian, he can still get married. His right to vote is determined by state law, and in some states, people determined to be "incompetent" cannot vote. However, your child may still be able to vote if he has a legal guardian. Your child must pass a written test and a driving test to prove himself competent to drive, but having a legal guardian does not mean that your child can't have a driver's license. Becoming a legal guardian can be a lengthy process, so you should consult a lawyer before your child turns 18, if possible.

REFLECTIONS ON PARENTING

It can be difficult to assess and predict your child's next steps after high school. Services for young adults with autism drop off after high school, so it is critical to begin planning for this transition well in advance of your child's high school graduation date. Working with your child's teachers, you want to look realistically at your child's goals and help him or her move toward independence and young adulthood.

It can be difficult to imagine your child living on his own, and it can be hard to trust that he will have the wherewithal to do so at times. However, there are options that can make you and your child feel more comfortable about his ability to enter adult life, including a supportive college program or a residential program that helps give young adults the social and practical skills they need to live on their own. The preparation for independent living can be a long and considered process, and it may also involve significant financial burdens for you and your family. However, this long process can be less confusing and painful if it involves your child and trusted professionals, including teachers, therapists, and possibly lawyers, who can guide you.

PARENTING STRATEGIES

- If possible, involve your teen in helping formulate the transition goals in her IEP, so that the goals are more relevant to her and she will be more invested in the outcome.

- When deciding which level of support your child needs in college, assess whether he can advocate for his needs. If not, he is unlikely to be successful in a relatively unstructured college program.

- Resources permitting, consider options that will allow your young adult to live outside the home in a structured or community-based program that can help him develop college-readiness or independent-living skills.

- Consider enrolling your young adult child in dual-enrollment programs so she can begin to take college courses while still receiving the support of services provided in high school.

8

Self-Care for Parents

Trinity found it hard to watch the children at the school where she taught. Her son had been diagnosed with autism was he was 2, and he struggled with aggressive behavior and learning to speak. When Trinity watched the verbal, happy boys and girls at the school where she taught kindergarten, she couldn't help but wish things were different for her son. What she imagined his life would be when he was born was very different from what it was now, and she sought help from a pastoral counselor to cope with her feelings of loss.

When her son was first diagnosed with high-functioning autism, Liz attended support groups for parents but did not feel comfortable sharing her story with others, as she was a single parent and did not feel that she had much in common with people facing autism as couples. She later found a therapist, paid for by her insurance, who she felt comfortable speaking to about her family and her son's issues.

Jack felt explosive toward his son, Jasper, who disrupted family meals and refused to do his homework. By signing up for a parenting mindfulness class, he found ways to practice compassion and stay in the moment with his son. Though he still had moments when he became enraged and had to walk away, he found that overall, he was calmer and better able to be attentive to his son's—and his own—needs.

CARING FOR SPECTRUM KIDS: COPING STRATEGIES

This chapter presents practical and psychological strategies to help parents care for themselves as their children age through adolescence into young adulthood and beyond. Though programs that help families with autism are primarily aimed at children, it's also essential for parents to get support to be in the best position to help their children and to bolster their own physical and mental health. Although parents often get lost in the equation, they shouldn't be. Your well-being is critical to the functioning of your child and your family.

This is the last chapter in the book, but it is by no means an afterthought. Your ability to care for your child is affected by your health, and keeping yourself healthy, mentally and physically, and socially connected, is vital to helping your child. However, this is easier said than done, as our society does not always make care and support for families with children with disabilities a priority. Some states provide more care and services than others (see Chapter 5), and a lack of respite care across the country affects parents and caregivers of children with autism. Our society's lack of support for families trying to raise a child with autism makes it very hard on parents, and if you feel depressed, it's totally understandable. There's not a lot of practical or emotional support for people with autism and their families, and the cost of raising a child with autism can be another compounding factor. Much of what more progressive countries (and some states in the U.S.) might provide as government services must be covered by parents themselves, such as ABA (applied behavior analysis) services. In addition, parents on the brink of retirement, or who are caring for elderly parents or other relatives, must also shoulder the expense of caring for adult children with autism.

Research published in the *Review Journal of Autism and Developmental Disorders* by Wei Wei Lai and colleagues has established that the chronic stress associated with being a caregiver for a child with a disability can affect the mental and physical health of the caregivers. This probably comes as no surprise to parents raising kids on the spectrum. Caring for a child with a disability can lead to disruption in the family and to social isolation. This is particularly true if your child shows aggressive or disruptive behaviors, and isolation seems like the only solution for keeping your child and others safe. The unfortunate and ironic effect is that caregivers and parents need more, rather than less, support to help their children.

In addition, parents may be mourning their loss of traditional parenting roles and activities, and this is understandable, too. It can be hard to watch your child's siblings, cousins, or other children in the neighborhood go through childhood rites of passage, such as having birthday parties and graduations, when you know that your child can't go through these rituals in the same way. This loss can result in a long process of mourning.

The ways in which parents cope with the stresses of raising a child with autism vary and are partially dependent on their culture and resources. For example, the study mentioned previously by Wei found that Asian parents might tend to favor collective responses to coping, whereas European parents might favor more individual responses. Understanding one's cultural and family values is essential to finding the right kind of coping mechanisms and support.

Studies on coping among caregivers and parents of children with autism spectrum disorder (ASD) have found that social support was the most helpful in stressful times. Other helpful strategies included family integration, cooperation, being optimistic, maintaining one's self-esteem and psychological stability, and having the help of a professional to understand a child. In a review of the literature, Wei and other researchers found that what they called "emotion-focused" coping, which involved denial, wishful thinking, and disengagement (such as by removing oneself by going to work), resulted in higher levels of parents' and caregivers' depression, stress, and anxiety. Parents and caregivers had lower levels of depression, stress, and anxiety when they used active or problem-solving coping strategies, including planning, seeking social support, and cognitive reframing.

Cognitive reframing, a technique borrowed from cognitive behavioral therapy, can be especially helpful. It involves changing the way you look at events, even if you can't change the events themselves. In many ways, people can shift how they see events, and their perspective is more critical than the events themselves.

Consider the following scenario. Louisa has collected knick-knacks for years. She asks for them as presents for her birthday and holidays, and they've begun to clutter her small house. Her son, Jamie, started to become aggressive at age 12, breaking several of her prized possessions and forcing her to put away others. Some she decided to give away as gifts. Here are two ways she can regard this scenario:

- She mourns the loss of her knickknacks and feels bitter each day that she looks at her empty shelves.

- She realizes that she shouldn't be so tied to her material possessions, and she believes that her living room looks better without the clutter.

Though Louisa faced the same situation in both scenarios, she interpreted them differently, and this type of reframing can be helpful to parents and caregivers of people with autism. On the other hand, comparing one's child with typically developing children is a natural inclination, but this type of wishful thinking and what-ifs can lead to depression and stress.

FINDING SUPPORT

Finding support is incredibly beneficial for parents of kids on the spectrum, but it can be difficult. Some parents prefer to find support from the teachers and professionals who work with their child, and others are more comfortable finding support from community or autism networks and support groups.

There is no one right way to find support. When you are facing a crisis with your child, it's very common for relatives and friends, though they are well meaning, to assume or tell you that you should get support in certain ways. However, the way you find help and emotional support is up to you and must be something you feel comfortable with. Autism Speaks has a list of support groups in different states, for both people with autism and caregivers, and they also have resources for people who want to incorporate different religions into their support network (see the Appendix for more information).

YOUR COMMUNITY

It is not rare for parents of autistic kids to receive calls from Child Protective Services (CPS). Barring situations of actual abuse, this is the worst misuse of these types of services and shows a true misunderstanding of teenagers and adults with ASD. It is clear, from anecdotes others have shared, that the staff at most CPS centers and agencies are not trained to understand autism, and neighbors or other people will call these services when a child with autism elopes or is dysregulated in public places.

It can help parents if they inform their neighbors and even the local police about their child and his or her needs. It can be helpful if you keep your child's records on hand, including his diagnosis, a statement from his doctor, and a record of his medications. That way, if the police or CPS are called, you can hopefully dispatch with the case quickly and without result. If your child is able to go out on his own, he should carry a laminated card with information about his autism. Although the police and people in the community are not always well informed about autism, this situation is changing. Some police departments have even formulated policies about how to work with people with autism, and the community at large is becoming more aware of autism (especially now that characters with autism are featured in TV shows and movies, and even on *Sesame Street*).

It's natural to want to isolate yourself and your family from members of the community, but you might also be preventing yourself from receiving support. By letting neighbors know about your child, you might find some sympathetic support. As rates of autism are rising quickly, many people have a friend or relative with autism, and they can either provide you with help (such as doing errands or accompanying you and your child on outings in the community) or with understanding.

More and more community organizations also offer support and open times for people on the spectrum and their caregivers. For example, Chuck E. Cheese, at the time of publication, was offering Sensory Sensitive Sundays on the first Sunday of each month in some locations so that the experience is friendlier to the senses of kids on the spectrum (they also open earlier so that the space is less crowded). Many trampoline places also offer times that are specifically open to spectrum kids and their parents. Some houses of worship also offer sensory-sensitive services.

MINDFULNESS-BASED PARENTING

Studies by a researcher named Elisabeth Dykens and colleagues have shown that positive psychology and mindfulness-training-based programs can help reduce the stress, depression, and anxiety and improve the life satisfaction and sleep of mothers of children with disabilities. In addition, mindfulness-based parenting strategies have shown to be effective for mothers of children with ADHD (attention-deficit/hyperactivity disorder) and ODD (oppositional defiant disorder). These results would also likely be applicable to fathers and other caregivers, too. As the authors of the study of children with ADHD noted, parents of children with disruptive behaviors often wind up devoting their attention to these disruptive behaviors and often respond in their children in impulsive ways that are referred to as "overreactive."

Mindful parenting techniques apply the principles of mindfulness, of staying in the moment, to the interaction with children. Practitioners pay attention to their thoughts and feelings while staying present in the moment. The basic idea is for parents to remain nonjudgmental and open and to be less reactive as they interact with their children. In addition, parents are encouraged to practice their own meditation daily to reduce their own stress and create harmony in the family. The training often begins with training to focus on sensations in one's body and breathing and builds to psychoeducation about one's overreactivity with one's child and to working on the parent–child interaction. Children also work on their own self-control through mindfulness, and the sessions are usually taught by cognitive behavioral therapists.

Learning this type of parenting practice is not easy, but with practice, parents can try to listen to children while paying full attention to them, can practice compassion for themselves and their child, and can accept their reality—and that of the child—without bias. As mentioned previously, mindfulness training can help people reduce the connections between the amygdala, the emotional center of the brain, and other areas of the brain, so that people can respond in less reactive ways and in ways that involve greater self-regulation. This type of stress reduction, which is offered by autism support groups, can be critical for parents who spend a great deal of their time caring for the needs of their children.

FOSTERING THE STRENGTHS OF ASD KIDS AND PARENTS

Positive psychology, which has also been shown to be effective in reducing the stress levels of parents with disabilities, emphasizes health and well-being rather than dysfunction. Started by Martin Seligman, positive psychology focuses on the skills that encourage flourishing rather than just on curing mental disorders and helps people develop love and compassion, creativity, and integrity.

Positive psychology can offer strategies for parents and young people with autism to move away from negativity and embrace their strengths. Rather than concentrating on the "deficits model" of disability—that autism is an all-round disability and indicates a lack of essential skills and strengths—a positive psychology approach can help parents and people with autism see the strengths in themselves and their relationships. These strengths can be fostered through a good fit between the individual and his surroundings, including his family, school, and community. Research has shown that ASD children with supportive environments, as well as positive interaction in the community, can thrive. In the years ahead, it will be necessary not only to continue to refine our knowledge of what can help kids with ASD and their families on an individual level, but also to build in community support, such as programs that match ASD youth to typically developing peers, to help ASD kids, teens, and adults to thrive. As people with ASD have clear strengths and talents, it will be a loss not only to them and their families but also to their communities if more systemic help is not put into place.

STRATEGIES FOR TAKING CARE OF YOURSELF

- Be compassionate to yourself. You are not superhuman. Raising children on the spectrum can result in serious parental stress, depression, and anxiety—but help is available.

- Try active coping strategies, such as cognitive reframing, finding support, and planning.

- Connect with members of the community and find resources in your community that are autism friendly to feel less stressed and find additional forms of support.

- Consider getting individualized support, such as therapy, or joining a support group, as resources and your comfort levels allow.

- Mindful parenting techniques can help you relate to your own experience, and to that of your child, with compassion and less stress.

- Remember that YOU deserve help and support, just as your children do!

Parent Resources

WEBSITES

- Autism Speaks (http://www.autismspeaks.org) is an advocacy organization that provides helpful and informative articles about autism and raising kids with autism from infancy to adulthood. They provide helpful kits and downloadable guides to help spectrum kids in situations such as going to the dentist or taking a shower and information about how to navigate the IEP process.

- Autism in Black (http://www.autisminblack.com/medical.html) provides more information about autism in the African American community.

- The Color of Autism (http://www.thecolorofautism.org/programs) offers resources and programs to help African Americans in the autism community.

- Behavior Analyst Certification Website (https://www.bacb.com) helps you find an ABA therapist in your area.

- Commonsense Media (http://www.commonsensemedia.org) helps parents understand the violence level, language, and other features of video games.

- Cooking With Autism (http://www.cookingwithautism.com) offers cooking classes tailored to people with autism and Asperger's Syndrome and publishes a book called *Coach in the Kitchen* with recipes tested to work well for chefs with gross or fine motor issues, food sensitivities and sensory issues, and problems following multi-step directions.

- Story Board That (http://www.storyboardthat.com) provides social stories on dating and safety presented with characters who represent diversity.

- Social Thinking (https://www.socialthinking.com) helps people develop social competencies.

- Spectrum News (http://www.spectrumnews.org) provides the latest news about medical breakthroughs and scientific studies about autism in terms parents can understand. There is a weekly newsletter to which you can subscribe.

- Think College (https://thinkcollege.net) provides college options for students with intellectual disabilities.

- Twainbow (https://twainbow.org) is an organization to support people who live under the double rainbow as people with autism who are also lesbian, gay, bisexual, or transgender.

- UC Davis's Mind Institute (http://www.ucdmc.ucdavis.edu) provides information about assistive technology to help people with communication.

BOOKS AND VIDEOS

Atwood, T. (2008). *The complete guide to Asperger's Syndrome.* London, United Kingdom: Jessica Kingsley.

Atwood, T., Grandin, T., Bolick, T., Faherty, C., Iland, L., McIlwee Myers, J., . . . Wrobel, M. (2006). *Asperger's and girls.* Arlington, TX: Future Horizons.

Baron-Cohen, S. (1997). *Mindblindness: An essay on autism and theory of mind.* Cambridge, MA: A Bradford Book.

Baron-Cohen, S. (2004). *The essential difference: Male and female brains and the truth about autism.* New York, NY: Basic Books.

Cook O'Toole, J. (2012). *The Asperkids' (secret) book of social rules: The handbook of not-so-obvious social guidelines for tweens and teens with Asperger Syndrome.* London, United Kingdom: Jessica Kingsley.

Grandin, T. (2006). *Thinking in pictures: My life with autism.* New York, NY: Vintage.

Grossberg, B. (2012). *Asperger's rules: How to make sense of school and friends*. Washington, DC: Magination Press.

Grossberg, B. (2015). *Asperger's and adulthood: A guide to working, loving, and living with Asperger's Syndrome*. Berkeley, CA: Althea Press.

Grossberg, B. (2015). *Asperger's teens: Understanding high school for students on the autism spectrum*. Washington, DC: Magination Press.

Harris, S. L., & Glasberg, B. A. (2003). *Siblings of children with autism: A guide for families* (2nd ed.). Bethesda, MD: Woodbine House.

Hoopmann, K. (2006). *All cats have Asperger Syndrome*. London, United Kingdom: Jessica Kingsley.

Hoopmann, K. (2015). *Blue bottle mystery: An Asperger adventure*. London, United Kingdom: Jessica Kingsley.

Mahler, K. J. (2009). *Hygiene and related behaviors for children and adolescents with autism spectrum and related disorders: A fun curriculum with a focus on social understanding*. Shawnee Mission, KS: AAPC.

Prince-Hughes, D. (Ed.). (2002). *Aquamarine blue: Personal stories of college students with autism*. Athens, OH: Swallow Press.

Robison, J. E. (2008). *Look me in the eye: My life with Asperger's*. New York, NY: Three Rivers Press.

Robison, J. E. (2014). *Raising Cubby: A father and son's adventures with Asperger's, trains, tractors, and high explosives*. New York, NY: Broadway Books.

Saperstein, J. A. (2014). *Getting a life with Asperger's: Lessons learned on the bumpy road to adulthood*. New York, NY: Penguin.

Shore, S., Naseef, R. (Contributors), & Gottlieb, D. (Moderator). (2009). *Living along the autism spectrum: What does it mean to have autism or Asperger Syndrome* [DVD]? Shawnee Mission, KS: AAPC.

Silverman, S. M., Kenworthy, L., & Weinfeld, R. (2014). *School success for kids with high-functioning autism*. Waco, TX: Prufrock Press.

Simone, R. (2010). *Asperger's on the job: Must-have advice for people with Asperger's or high functioning autism and their employers, educators, and advocates*. Arlington, TX: Future Horizons.

Simone, R. (2010). *Aspergirls: Empowering females with Asperger Syndrome*. London, United Kingdom: Kingsley.

Smith Myles, B., Endow, J., & Mayfield, M. (2012). *The hidden curriculum of getting and keeping a job: Navigating the social landscape of employment—A guide for individuals with autism spectrum and other social-cognitive challenges*. Shawnee Mission, KS: AAPC.

Verdick, E., & Reeve, E. (2012). *The survival guide for kids with autism spectrum disorders (and their parents)*. Minneapolis, MN: Free Spirit.

Index

About the Author

Blythe Grossberg, PsyD, is a learning specialist who works with children, teens, and young adults on the autism spectrum to help them function more effectively in school and achieve their potential. She is the author of *Asperger's Rules, Asperger's Teens* (winner of a Gold Medal from the Mom's Choice Awards), and *Asperger's and Adulthood.*

PARENTING

If you have a child with autism spectru⬚⬚⬚⬚⬚⬚⬚⬚⬚⬚⬚⬚⬚⬚⬚⬚⬚⬚⬚⬚er through the teenage years to adulthood is often rewarding but may also be complicated, confusing, and financially challenging. The scientifically validated guidance that Blythe Grossberg offers in this book can help you during this journey. Grossberg provides supportive advice for finding good medical and psychiatric care, helping your teen learn executive functioning and social skills to navigate middle and high school, and talking with your teen about sexual development and sexual activity. You will also find helpful resources for college and transition programs, as well as ideas for taking care of yourself throughout this stage of your parenting adventure.

Many parents of adolescents with ASD will likely identify with the challenges that Grossberg describes in this book. She breaks downs these challenges in a clear, readable manner and provides practical and useful strategies. Anyone who interacts with adolescents with ASD will benefit from this book.

—**MICHELLE L. PALUMBO, MD,** Lurie Center for Autism at Massachusetts General Hospital for Children, Lexington

About the Author

BLYTHE GROSSBERG, PsyD, is a learning specialist who works with children, teens, and young adults with ASD to help them function more effectively in school and achieve their potential. She is the author of *Asperger's Rules, Asperger's Teens* (gold medal winner from the Mom's Choice Awards), and *Asperger's and Adulthood.*

APA LifeTools is an imprint of the American Psychological Association, the largest scientific and professional organization representing psychology in the United States and the largest association of psychologists worldwide.
http://www.apa.org/pubs/books/lifetools

$19.99

ISBN 9781433830150

90000 >

**AMERICAN
PSYCHOLOGICAL
ASSOCIATION**

750 First Street, NE
Washington, DC 20002
www.apa.org

9 781433 830150